THE MANAGERS BATHROOM BOOK

"Things you can learn in one sitting"

Jay Andres

LeNoble Publishing
NV Design

In Praise of *The Managers Bathroom Book*

Knowing the author as a friend and mentor, we have spent hours discussing leadership, team culture, recruitment, stakeholder relations, communication and so many more subjects. As a young manager this book couldn't have come at a better time. The book offers true pearls of wisdom that can only be developed via experience. I find myself constantly referring to the book for help in tricky situations and have been able to implement a lot of the advice directly.

Michael Poole
General Manager
Doha, Qatar

I found "The Managers Bathroom Book" about 25 years too late. In each chapter I saw bits and pieces of myself and the mistakes I made in my management journey. The Email Tips chapter should be required reading for every business leader. The Managers Bathroom Book is an easy and fun read and is a "MUST HAVE" for any manager... young or old. Well done Jay Andres!

John Gilliam
Regional Operations Manager – Coinstar

I had the privilege to work with and learn from Jay for almost a decade. Jay's natural curiosity, penchant for analytics and, results-oriented mindset make him a force to be reckoned with in the business world and beyond. This book is a testament to his achievements and an invaluable resource that will resonate with a diverse audience in its pursuit of continuous improvement and journey of learning.

Davorin Todorovac
Vice President of Finance
Primo Water LLC

"Did I ever tell you the story..."; this is the line I heard Jay say almost daily when I had the fortune of working for him. The stories often provided a practical solution to a problem. This bathroom book is more than a collection of experiences, observations, and stories collected over time; it is his smorgasbord of insights that cautions, encourages and provides perspective to young and aspiring managers. Between the lines, one can sense the presence of a candid and experienced coach that can relate to the day-to-day obstacles we face and overcome as Leaders of or within an organization.

Alexander van t 'Riet
Chief Executive Officer
Mai Dubai Bottled Water

Published by LeNoble Publishing, Designed by NV Design LLC
First Edition, Second Printing

ISBN: 978-1-955132-08-4

Dedication

This book is dedicated to Marvin Andres, Joe, Bob, Kourtney,
John, Willie, Simon, Bill B, Bill L, Ray S, Greg, Chris, Kent,
Dennis, Mike, Pete, Gordon, Tom, Mike, Fady, Waleed, Saeed
and
Ruth Andres

Almost all my bosses

CONTENTS

INTRODUCTION

Let me start by telling you how this book came about. During my 45 plus years of working, I spent 38 years in Leadership. I had the good fortune of working for some very good leaders. I was also lucky in the fact that my direct exposure to working for bad leaders was limited. Although there were a few.

The best ones passed on their knowledge and led by example as well. I always appreciated the fact that someone would invest the time to teach me how to do something as opposed to those who would just tell me to go do it.

As time went on and I gained experience as well as expertise, I thoroughly enjoyed developing my skills as well as the skills of those I worked with.

I loved learning and admired great leaders. My reading habits for years included two categories of books. Business books about leadership and communication and recreational reading, about Leaders. Many of which were Biographies.

I also found that I enjoyed putting my thoughts in writing. I enjoyed that form of expression.

In terms of my work history, my second job in life ended up being my career. That was in 1979 in Los Angeles working for Sparkletts Bottled Drinking Water.

I first applied in 1974 and was rejected. I came back 5 years later and started as a Relief Driver. The very bottom. During my 31 years there, I was promoted 6 times with my final position being Vice President and General Manager of the largest Region in the Country.

My career progression resulted in 5 corporate relocations and managing locations in 8 Western States.

I attempted retirement after 31 years and was not very good at it. As a result, I accepted a job in the United Arab Emirates in Dubai. While there, I was recruited by the Government of Dubai to start a bottled water company from scratch.

That story is deserving of its own book. In a paragraph, it went like this....

When I started it, all we had was a brand name. Mai Dubai Bottled Water. When I retired from Mai Dubai after 8 years, we had close to 1,100 employees, 4 Distribution Centers, a 420,000 square foot factory which was viewed by industry experts as the most advanced bottled water factory in the industry, with revenue of $70,000,000 and a small profit.

On more than one occasion, I was asked, "Have you ever thought of writing a book?" My standard answer was "I like writing, so yeah, maybe someday I will do that". The feedback in this regard included examples of where my advice had an impact, not just in terms of strategic decisions, but more importantly the development of those I worked around.

During my first attempted (1 year) retirement, I started the book. Over the next 10 years, I would periodically revisit it to adjust and add to the contents. On occasion, I would pull a chapter out and give it to someone that I thought might benefit from it.

Some other questions you might have:

How did you select the material? The contents are a combination of common topics as well as what I believe is somewhat obscure. For instance, Common = Listening Obscure = How to resist a bad idea and survive. My goal is to help you become a better Manager. I believe the process of growing includes a whole bunch of small things in terms of skill-building and a few big things. This book covers mostly what would be considered small things like email and few big things, like Managing your boss. And the book only includes stuff that I have had experience in.

Why did you choose that title? Or put another way, why the push for brevity? Our preferred method of learning differs from one individual to the next. In today's environment, we are barraged with information. Even, when we are attempting to relax, we can bet someone or something is attempting to teach us! We have only been taking phones into the bathroom with us for about 15 years. This book will appeal to those who enjoy multitasking. In my opinion multi-taskers clutter up their efforts to distract themselves. If they are executing against two tasks at the same time, you can be assured that they feel one of the tasks is more important than the other. The boring task needs to be supplemented with one that gets their attention. I made every attempt to be concise and to summarize the subject in just a few pages. Not enough to make you an expert, however, it should provoke thought and hopefully action. To that end, the Managers bathroom book was designed.

How should I use/read this book? I believe the book is written in such a way that it can be read cover to cover, back to front, or by randomly selecting chapters. There are no pre-requisites, although you might be advised to read a chapter that relates to the chapter you are currently reading, to reinforce the message. You might use it for a reference-based upon what you are faced at work with on any given day. It's not a summer beach read that will keep you mesmerized for hours on end. I have tried in many instances to bullet point the contents of a chapter and also bold the key phrases.

A lot of what we learn is through osmosis. We are not always aware that we are in the midst of learning. Our opinion of how to win at work is created by a variety of experiences and influences. This book hopefully helps you learn something or at a minimum exercise the brain so that you are susceptible to learning.

Sometimes, this and other books help us realize something that we did not know that we knew. I suppose this is the cousin of a more famous saying "I don't know, what I don't know".

It's my hope and experience that some (not all) of the following advice will resonate with you and contribute to the ongoing process of learning that is part of each Manager's lifelong process of becoming a Leader.

CHAPTER ONE

RESISTING A BAD IDEA (AND SURVIVING)

Let me start with a couple of qualifying paragraphs on the high-risk act of resisting a bad idea. If you do not feel confident in your position, you should simply skip this chapter as it might tempt you to resist before you are ready. It is essential that you feel a sense of security regarding the opinion of those that matter in terms of your value to your company.

Mind you, resisting is a more aggressive stance than simply seeking clarity, voicing doubt, or even exhibiting apathy, which is a passive-aggressive technique that usually does not work in either derailing a bad idea or adding to your worth as an Associate.

The soundest advice I ever received in this area was early in my career and has been often repeated. "Choose your battles". As a new Manager, you will tend to be idealistic and interested in "Changing the world". As a seasoned veteran Manager, you will have an altruistic sense that you need to "save the company" from those evil-doers with bad ideas.

The danger in resisting, and make no mistake, it can be dangerous, is the impact it can have on your reputation. Consider the possible options and perception of your resistance.

• Despite your resistance, the idea is launched and is a resounding success. You are on your way to being viewed as the companies Anti-Christ and future resistance may actually accelerate the launch of a bad idea.

• Despite your resistance, the idea is launched and is a dismal failure. You are at least partially blamed for the failure because you are viewed as resisting from start to finish. You may even be accused either publicly or privately of being a saboteur.

I must admit that there were some ideas that I viewed as bad, that ultimately turned out to be anywhere from good to very good. So be very careful in your assessment. Generally, we should all be open to new ideas, even if they failed in the past. Some of the greatest ideas fail miserably the first time they are attempted.

You can ask a few short questions to determine if an idea has the potential to be in the "Bad" category.

1. Does the idea fail to keep the customer in the crosshairs? Will your customers actually suffer upon implementation of the plan?

2. If it was tried in the past and failed miserably, has something changed either in the Market or in the execution plan to ensure success?

3. Is the plan being pushed by someone with a track record of success and what appears to be their true motive?

4. Is the plan considering aspects of the change model in terms of securing buy-in from your companies Associates first, followed by your customers?

5. Whose idea, is it? Quite frankly, if it happens to be the CEO's Pet Project and you are more than one layer away in terms of a reporting relationship, you will want to be extremely careful. While many companies have an atmosphere where you can disagree with those above you, one should proceed with caution as this is not always the case. Put another way, it is a fast way to shorten your career, so you better be right.

Let's assume that you have a strong conviction about something you describe as a bad idea, and you have a strong reputation that has been attained via both your results and your relationships, here are some pointers.

1. **Appear open to the idea.** Watch your body language, facial
    expressions, and any other non-verbal expressions. You may even
    want to voice some vocal support for the idea. Of course, you need
    to be ethical and not lie, however, find something positive within
    the idea to support. If nothing else you can support the goal of the
    idea, which typically is intended to improve some function of the
    company's performance. This may cause others to believe that you
    are taking a pragmatic approach to the idea and cause them to be
    more open to listening to the concerns that you bring up.

2. **Be sure you can articulate the rationale behind your resistance
    in an intelligent manner.** Simply saying "This will never work" or
    "we tried that before and it bombed" will only elicit an aggressive
    push from the idea owner. Make an attempt to quantify the risk
    in either dollars or the hard-to-measure categories of image,
    morale, and distraction to the organization. In today's competitive
    environment there is a necessary shift towards taking risks in an
    effort to compete. While we must be bold and exhibit courage
    in our approach to "making the number" we must guard against
    being either reckless or stupid.

3. **Do not announce your resistance.** Ask lots of questions. The
    answers or lack of answers will nurture any doubt that exists. Who
    knows, it may actually lead your group to an alternative solution.

4. **Look for allies.** Do not interpret this tip as advice to mounting
    a conspiracy or organizing resistance. Simply be on the lookout
    for those who may either share your point of view or have some
    level of doubt. Dig deeper with those individuals. Your collective
    thoughts may begin to gain momentum within the group, and
    you will not be that lone voice in the wilderness anymore! In this
    case, silence does not necessarily signal compliance or agreement.
    Attempt to subtly pull those silent types into the conversation.

5. **Whenever possible, offer an alternative solution.** Doubters or
    Resistors can be viewed in a positive light if they are offering
    up other ideas. Especially when those ideas prove to be better
    than the original plan. A win-win approach is to suggest a

modified approach, which has elements of the "bad idea" as well as adjustments, that will improve the likelihood of success.

6. **Determine your tolerance for pain in advance of your actions to resist.** Know how far you are willing to go in terms of your resistance level. If you feel you have built up some equity in terms of your reputation, you may feel you can go pretty far in terms of your resistance. Knowing this in advance may prevent you from driving off a cliff during an emotional exchange on the subject. It is easy to say, "I would bet my career on this." You may sound brave; however, it is almost never a good idea to lay it all on the line in an effort to prevail. Someone might take you up on the wager.

7. **When communicating to the decision-maker or sponsor of the idea, particularly when they are higher up the ladder than you, make every attempt to limit public resistance.** Once you are ultra-prepared and informed, it is better to attempt a one-on-one conversation if that opportunity exists. Some Leaders will resist public concessions at all costs. While they likely possess misguided principles it is more important for them to win than to be accurate.

8. **Don't attack.** Suggest, propose, request, seek consideration. If you can somehow make them think that a change to the plan or an alternative plan is their idea, all the better. Some examples of how to tactfully serve these ideas up are;

   a. Have you considered…

   b. I like the idea in many ways and am glad you are pushing this initiative. I am sure you have considered every possibility. Can you explain how we are going to overcome the obstacle of…

   c. When I look at this plan, I see many positives, and just a couple of obstacles to overcome which I would like to discuss with you.

    d. Everything is great about this idea, except the timing. I believe the success of the project will improve if we delay it until...

9. **If you feel the idea will seriously damage the company, (not just your part of it) prepare to graphically articulate your opinion with facts presented in a convincing manner.** Again, easier said than done, and at this point only you can determine if you want this just to be one-on-one, public, or both.

10. **If your resistance is ineffective and the plan proceeds, you better jump on board and find a way to support it.** Be very careful about sharing your doubts with those below you. Work very hard at executing the plan and bite your tongue in terms of ongoing criticism. If it does fail, do not gloat. If it succeeds, admit you are wrong and have learned from the experience. There is power in being contrite in these instances.

If you hit a brick wall of resistance it is likely that either one of you, or both of you have gotten to the emotional state. If that be the case, circle back after a cooling-off period that might be a few hours, but not more than a few days. In that follow-up meeting re-affirm your loyalty to the organization if not the bad idea holder. Thank him or her for listening! Thank them also for their openness to hear dissent and to also get past a disagreement. Approach this portion of the process with humility, leave the door open, but don't insist on further discussion.

Realize that as you climb the corporate ladder your individual resistance will have more force. At the same time, you must realize that few are able to move up in an organization if they are resisting on a regular basis. However, if you show courage and your input helps your Company, you will be recognized for your intelligent approach and advanced business acumen.

Probably not a good idea to share this chapter with those higher-up decision-makers that you are attempting to resist!

CHAPTER TWO

SUCKING UP – IT CAN WORK, BUT NOT FOREVER

This is one chapter where you will find only a small amount of advice or tips directly related to the subject matter. It will however help you understand and identify Suck-ups that you will undoubtedly come across throughout your work life. The chapter may help you understand who you are, in this regard and maybe even who you want to be.

Let's start with the terminology. Suck-up is a rather crass and unsophisticated jargon used to identify someone who is trying to survive or advance simply by letting the boss know how much they are loved and admired by the Suck-up. While there are other suitable terms such as a Brown Noser, Kiss Ass, Yes Man, Sycophant, Human Suppository, Suck Boy, and Suck Butt, Suck-up is as good as any.

I once inherited a workgroup, that had as a member one of the company's more famous Suck-ups. We will call him Dan. Dan's previous Manager had abruptly retired if you know what I mean?

Dan was the first Supervisor to meet with me at one of my new locations. After some insincere compliments directed towards his new object of affection, me, he launched into an emotional description of his feelings. He was deeply saddened by the departure of his previous manager. He said "I am devastated by Howie's departure. I had worked very hard at establishing a relationship with him. I worked very hard to please him and now it's all down the drain. I must start over". I explained, "Managers come and go and while there is nothing wrong with establishing a relationship with your boss, your focus should be on yourself and your results when it comes to preparing for the next step up".

The guy was ultimately promoted. Not by me, but by someone else who was a bit more susceptible to his approach than I was. Ultimately his lack of substance and poor results caught up with him, resulting in his termination.

I would be the first to admit that there is a fine line between Sucking Up and being Politically Astute. Let's face it, we have all found ourselves in positions where we might have gone a little bit past being politically astute for a few minutes or weeks. Think of the last time you were a member of a workgroup that experienced some level of regime change. If you had to choose between sucking up a little bit and being the person who told the new Boss everything that was wrong with the company, within five minutes of a meeting, I hope you chose the former approach.

My experience has allowed me to observe three distinct categories of Sucking Up. Some Suck-ups migrate back and forth between categories, while some progress through the hierarchy as a result of perceived success at a lower level of sucking and their belief that "more is better" when it comes to showing the boss how much they are loved.

While Suck-ups may be born into any one of the categories, they often start out at level one and get to level three over time.

> **Level One Suck-ups** – The Silent Suck-up: These folks are often, hard to recognize because the vast majority of their sucking is done behind the scenes. They still have a little bit of guilt about their behavior and do not have the same level of conviction as level two and three Suck Ups. As a result, they will not be quite as shameless in their compliments or votes of confidence. Much of their sucking is by proxy or subliminal. For instance, they seldom voice disagreement and they will somehow get their spouse/significant other to suck-up as well to both the Boss and the Boss's spouse. They are quick to volunteer for the worst tasks.

They may have some of the same attributes as the other levels however they have a clandestine approach to the application of their skill set. For instance, they will never disagree with the Boss in a meeting. They may voice some concern, doubt, or lack of confidence in an idea, privately, however, if this passive approach meets with any resistance, they will come on board quickly and use this incident to tell the Boss how much they learned from the exchange of opinions. This is the gateway category for many, and you can bet that they are watching and learning from the other Suck Ups. If you find a need to suck-up, try this approach first, it is far less embarrassing and easier to live down, over the long haul.

> **Level Two Suck-ups** – The Situational Suck-up: This suck-up is environmentally driven and is a bit erratic in his application of sucking up. Yes, it can indeed be confusing to the target of the Suck Up. He will turn it on and off based upon the circumstances and while he will drift between level one and level two, he will seldom panic and move to level three. He is more willing to Suck-up in Public as he feels he has balanced his sucking with periodic resistance. "Situational's" are often the people who agree in public, but in private and behind their back, they will tear down the boss. A Situational quickly assesses the risk versus benefit of his Sucking Up. Weighing the potential ridicule and loss of credibility with his peer group, against the potentially favorable impression he will make on those who are in power.

On the day that everyone meets the new leader, there will likely be a vortex created by all the sucking that goes on, this is the day that the Situational's come out of the woodwork. Be careful during these times as the Suck-ups tend to conflict with the egomaniacs who are working in overdrive to prove how knowledgeable and indispensable they are. It is a volatile mixture, and you are better off if you simply wait patiently on the sidelines for a few hours or days. Don't compete with them right now, let them do their thing and use this time to assess the new boss's resistance or lack thereof to sucking.

> **Level Three Suck-ups** – The Shameless Suck-up: This is the one you see in Sitcoms. He is almost a caricature of a real person.

Shameless Suck-ups are typically born, not made. They have been known to complement their Kindergarten teacher's attire on the first day of school. They have no boundaries. They will use all the tricks known to Suck-ups at every level. They are so convinced that sucking up should be part of the process that they surround themselves with Junior Suck-ups who are in training to follow them up the corporate ladder.

They will go out and buy the same exact briefcase as their Boss. And when they see you using the same exact case that was given to you by your staff as a present, they will accuse you of being a Suck-up. They will do this right in front of the boss if at all possible. They are devoted to the relationship and results are secondary. They have a clinical case of insecurity. There is no known cure for the Shameless Suck-up.

Why does sucking up work at least temporarily? We all seek some level of buy-in and affirmation. Leaders should have conviction about their beliefs, tactics, and strategies and we should be seeking some level of consensus. The risk is that we want this support so badly that it blinds us to the truth. Typically, our best leaders have the strongest personalities. Even if those who are a layer or two away from us, up or down the organizational chart does not fully agree with us, we want and need those closest to us to help us sustain the approach we are taking. Leadership can be lonely, and this loneliness can cause us to be fooled by even the Shameless Suck-up.

While it does not work forever, it can in fact work for a very long time. Even CEO's can be Suck-ups. Suck-ups who last the longest will also have other skills that coupled with their ability to suck-up, will carry them up the corporate ladder. The reason it does not work forever is that sooner or later, a Manager will be judged on their results. How they execute, how the organization views them, what they stand for, and if they are trusted.

The members of a Suck-ups workgroup will typically despise their boss. Even the Junior Suck-ups will one day turn on the Senior Suck-up. Suck-up boss's teams often break into two camps. The Suck-ups and Non-Suck-ups will on occasion go to war. Surprisingly the Non-

Suck-ups can often prevail. Mainly because Suck-ups are not a very loyal group. Not to their boss, their peers, or their staff.

Sucking up can indeed carry them a few steps further than they deserve, however when they fail, they fail big. Because their success is weighted towards insincere relationships, they are only one regime change away from a total meltdown. When it happens, those around them will run for cover and they will quickly be forgotten.

How do you tell if you're a suck-up? It is difficult to self-identify. Part and parcel to being a suck-up is a denial of the malady itself. I will list the correlated attributes of a non-suck-up, as well as the suck-up, so that you can go to a quiet place and contemplate which descriptors best depict your own persona. Remembering that almost all of us have some suck-up tendencies.

The Non-Suck-up typically...

- Is focused on results.

- Does not like suck-ups, although he may be fooled by those who suck-up to him

- Are sincere and truly care about people

- Tend to be loyal people. They want to be loyal to their Leader and they evoke loyalty from those they lead.

- Are self-confident

- Know who they are, and they are comfortable with their identity even if they are conscious of the need to improve themselves.

- Have loads of work ethic

- They support their boss but have built enough trust that they are able to disagree

- Seek personal and professional growth

- Have lasting and deep friendships

The Suck-up typically...

- Is almost solely focused on relationships with those above him. He will suck-up to a peer if he feels the peer is well-liked by the Boss.

- Does not like Suck-ups who are in competition with himself, however, loves surrounding himself with Suck-ups

- Are disingenuous. In severe instances, they take on evil qualities.

- Will turn on someone at the drop of a hat, even the former object of their affection.

- Have a clinical inferiority complex and are constantly seeking compliments.

- Have little self-awareness and are absolutely clueless about others opinion of them

- Is disconnected from the business and put so much effort into sucking up that they have little left for the job

- Blindly follow their Leader

- Seek only professional growth

- Have very few true friendships. Friendships are based upon what can be gained out of the friendship and not what can be given

The Suck-ups tendencies sound harsh, however, remember there are degrees of these attributes. My guess is that if you are not a suck-up, you know it. And if someone you work with or for, is a suck-up, you know that as well. It's you Suck-ups that will find this chapter useless.

So, what do you do when you encounter a suck-up? If they are a peer, stay out of their way. Do not let them drag you into their world where they can use you. Be cordial and cooperative, you do not want to make them your enemy, but do not trust them.

If the Suck-up happens to report to you and you see value in their future, you will want to address the issue with them. Start with the tactful approach and get more and more direct if they seem resistant to your approach. Build trust with them, so they can see that there are other ways to succeed. Keep your conversations focused on results and resist their attempts to get you to go golfing, camping, BBQing, and becoming Godfather to their children. The further they are along in the progression, the more direct and painful the conversation will be. You may only cure them temporarily. As I said, they are born and not made.

As a Leader, we need to be on guard in terms of being aware of Suck-ups who work for us. If you surround yourself with nothing but suck-ups, you are likely to go down the wrong path with your entire team and you are going to be insulated from the truth of how your organization feels about you and your ideas. Maybe this is why conquering Roman Generals placed a slave on their chariot when parading during their triumphant return from battle. This slave had one purpose and that was to whisper in the ear of the conqueror who was surrounded by would-be admirers, "You're only a man". At least that is what George C. Scott said in his role as Patton?

Who are you?

CHAPTER THREE

ADJUSTING TO YOUR NEW MANAGER"- SURVIVING REGIME CHANGE"

With rare exceptions, it is likely that you will work for several Managers throughout your career. Changes in who you will report to will be caused by a variety of actions. You may have chosen to move on to another company or location within your current company. Your Manager may choose to move on or find themselves promoted or asked to leave the Company. I said asked, but we know the truth!

There are two basic phases in the genesis of the Manager – Manager relationship. The first phase encapsulates the time frame, wherein the relationship is new. This is where the foundation is built and can be a make-or-break segment. This typically lasts no more than a year and can be as short as a few weeks.

During the second phase, there is either a level of trust that makes working together easier or there is a mood that is less than ideal. If the trust does not exist, the most you can hope for is the ability of both parties, too, at a minimum, to respect each other. Don't worry too much, it is not a certainty, that the relationship is doomed to failure, if you get into this second phase with a lack of trust, however the odds begin to shift in the wrong direction. Much like a marriage though, this situation can be salvaged.

With the ebb and flow of mergers and acquisitions, you may find yourself reporting to someone new because of a change in ownership.

Whatever the case, you will undoubtedly find yourself in a position where you have to adapt. Your ability to adjust will be most needed when there is a regime change that is a result of a perceived business need or results that are displeasing to the "higher-ups".

Let's list the basic causes for a change in management as there are some slight nuances to dealing with each of the changes.

1. You were promoted and are reporting to the Manager who supported your promotion and selected you.

2. Your new Manager followed what was perceived as a good Manager with good results.

3. Your new Manager followed what was perceived as a bad Manager with bad results.

It is difficult to hard code the advice in this area. You will need to again pick from the advice menu listed below. Those skills that are hopefully inherent in you will come into play, such as common sense, emotional intelligence, and your gut.

Regardless of the reason for you being in a position to be reporting to a new manager the following tips are useful in terms of surviving regime change.

1. **Concentrate on the future and not the past.** Face it, reporting to someone new or different can be unnerving. You may have just finished reporting to what you believe is the best Manager in the world. And while you have gotten over his or her departure you will find yourself longing for the good old days. If your former Manager were truly that good, he or she would want you to adapt quickly. You cannot adapt by living in the past. Focus on the present and the future and give the new guy a break. He or she has as many fears as you and will be looking for allies in those early days. Remembering that there are truly no secrets, and your new Manager probably already knows that you were loyal to the prior regime. If the prior Manager was eliminated for cause or poor performance guard against getting sucked into the vortex

that is circling the drain. You do not have to compromise your values to do this and attack your former Manager. Your focus on the present and future, along with consistent performance will send a message that you are moving on and want to be a part of this team.

2. **Concentrate on Listening** – It is likely that you will be competing with your peers for the Boss's ear. Depending on the circumstances related to the change, your fellow Managers may see this as either an opportunity or the worst thing that has ever happened to them. Some will act strangely as they attempt to prove themselves. Do not be like the exceptional athlete who day in and day out leads the league in statistics, but when it's time for the big game, they choke. Something goes wrong and it is usually because they are pressing. If you focus more attention on listening and observing early on, there is less likely that you will say or do something stupid. Much like investing, it is more critical to avoid the dumb mistake during this period than come up with a brilliant idea.

3. **Interview your New Manager** – Do not announce that you are conducting an interview. After all, you do not want to step out of bounds. This interview can and in most cases should, occur over the course of a few sessions. To ensure that it does not feel like an interview, do not have your list of questions in front of you. During the interview seek out areas where you have a common point of view. If you find some areas of significant disagreement, hold your tongue for now. Some good starter questions might be;

    a. **Do you have any pet peeves?** This lets your Manager know that you are willing and capable of adjusting to his or her needs or idiosyncrasies. Combined with other actions, you are sending the message that you are focused on the now and not the present. It may help you avoid a land mine as well.

    b. **How often do you want me to communicate with you? I may tend to over-communicate so please let me know if I am being a pest.** This may also open the door for how often you may need to hear from your boss. It again shows that you are proactive in your approach to adjusting to the new regime.

c. **What motivated you to promote-come to this company/ department** – Somewhat of a bold question to ask, so do not do it early on. This sends the message that you have a curiosity about yourself and that you are actually interested in your new Manager as a person. Good perceptions to have in most organizations.

d. **Tell me, what have been the keys to your success?** This is definitely an ego stroker, so be careful how you pull this arrow out of your quiver. Do not ask this one in your first session. This question communicates that you are interested in learning as well as potentially promoting yourself.

e. **What have been your observations in your first (fill in the blank) weeks in this position?**

f. **What is your favorite book? Or what is the last business book that you have read? Or what business books have made an impact on you?** There is a chance that your new boss is not a reader, or at least not a reader of books. It has been my observation that good Managers are readers, and the best ones are voracious readers. If you are asked this question back, be careful if you mention this book! Your Manager might go out and buy it (Not a bad thing for me) and reverse engineer your newfound approach to dealing with a new Manager. If you find that your Manager simply reads fiction, (Unless it is business fiction, yeah that's a thing) you will at least have learned to avoid this topic. You will also have learned that there is an opportunity to move past your Manager, at least in theoretical knowledge. Many businesspeople limit their reading to Biographies. I contend that biographies are indeed business books as they are essays on Leaders more often than not.

g. **Read His/ Her Favorite Book** – It is not enough to simply know what your managers favorite business book is. You need to read it! As you read it, attempt to discern those theories that are taught or supported in the book as well as by your managers actions. You may be able to have a deeper understanding and explanation of your manager style. I worked for a Senior Executive whose favorite book was a fictional account wherein the main character who provided solutions, did this simply by asking questions until the target of his questions figured it out. My manager approach was very similar. While the book did not expressly state it, he believed that the best way to develop was to figure it out yourself, or at least think you figured it out. In short, it will help you understand how your Manager ticks. If he finds out that you are reading his most favorite book, it will more than likely be taken as a compliment or endorsement of his Leadership approach.

h. Try to locate and network with one of your new Managers' former direct reports. They will likely have had a better understanding of your new boss. Be careful with this one, it will probably be reported to your Boss, which may or may not be a good thing. Regardless of their opinion of the Boss, good or bad, you will gain a deeper understanding of the makeup of your new Leader. At a minimum, I would hope your investigative efforts will be recognized.

Comments to avoid...

1. **I am interested in promoting** – While there will be a time for this comment, let your actions and reputation speak for you. If you are viewed by the organization as having potential, this subject will come up. It is certainly good to aspire, however, do not appear overanxious or desiring to promote for the wrong reasons.

2. **I am really glad you are here and happy they got rid of the prior Manager** – Even if this is true, this statement, particularly early in this new chapter of your career, is tacky. Comments like this lack ethics, at least the type of ethics I hope you want as part of your persona.

3. **I really loved the prior Manager and miss him or her dearly** – Again, even if it's true, a statement like this can only damage you.

You would think that a comment like this does not even need to be mentioned in this book, however, I have personally witnessed this comment. Yes, it was said to me when I replaced someone with abysmal results. And yes, this Manager did not last very long

4.   **Want to go golfing? Want to go have a beer? Want to come over Sunday for a BBQ?** I love that tie, where did you buy it? – Easy big fella, there will be a time and place for bonding, however, for now, let your new boss set the pace. Folks who do this are typically attempting to build and manage their relationship because they have not been managing their results. This type of exuberance puts your new Manager radar on high alert. My guess is, if this is your approach, you are probably not reading this type of book or any other books like it these days.

My formal work-life has encompassed 45 years and during that time I reported to 25 Managers even though I worked for the same company for 31 of those years. 22 of the 25 were anywhere from good to great and I learned from all of them.

Keep a positive attitude about the whole regime change process. If you get good at it, you not only evolve but find adaptation skills that are helpful in many other instances.

CHAPTER FOUR

MANAGING IN A CRISIS

If you have been in the workforce for more than a few years, you now know that a Crisis has some potential for good. This chapter will give you some pointers on how to maximize that potential.

Depending on your position in an organization, your role in a crisis will typically differ. You will either engage in an effort to fix the problem (Fixer), adapt to the problem (Adapter), or both fix and adapt. The role of Fixer/Adapter is usually held by those at the top of an Organization, Region, or Company.

The Fixer/Adapter may not actually do the work related to the fix or solution, however, he or she will be intimately involved in the discussions that lead up to the implementation phase, and while they may not do the heavy lifting associated with navigating out of the crisis, they will make and own the call-in terms of what is done to recover from the current circumstances.

Your primary role as a Leader in a crisis is mitigation. Depending on your span of control, influence, and experience, it is quite likely that your role will change and is likely to expand. Particularly if you are good at it. The cream rises to the top a lot faster in a crisis. At the same time, weakness is also revealed rather quickly.

Since the nature of a crisis typically crosses functions as well as departments and its scope can be wide-ranging, most of us find ourselves in the role of the Adapter. The following guiding principles apply to all of those involved in recovering during these trying times.

1. **First and foremost, make every effort to be visible.** While it is understandable that there will be more meetings and other activities that take you away from both your customers as well as your Associates, remember this is when they need you most. If the amount of time you have is diminished make sure it is impactful. If your organization is configured in such a way that it makes it difficult to be seen, then make sure you are heard by phone, one-on-one as well as conference calls. Fight the natural urge to run for cover. Lead from the front.

2. **Communicate until their ears bleed.** Let your Associates and Customers (if necessary) know what your plans are, or if it is too early for that, let them know that you are aware of the significance of the problem and are committed to finding a solution.

3. **Listen, listen, listen.** The forgotten component of the act of communicating. Make sure you are getting a clear understanding of the issues that are at the root of the crisis. In many cases, you may find the solution through this effort. At a minimum, you will discover some good tips in terms of implementing the solution.

4. **Burn some and build equity.** Hopefully, you have been in this particular position long enough to have built some trust and loyalty from those you lead. Ask them to be patient with you as you seek a solution. Be as candid as possible (you may have your Attorneys counseling you against this). Ask them to trust you and when the time comes, help you with the implementation of the measures you will need to take to resolve the crisis.

5. **Show confidence.** Assure everyone that you will find a way to overcome the obstacles and as a result become a better organization. You need to have a calmness in your voice. It is an old but appropriate saying "Do not let them see you sweat".

6. **Be an advocate for your Customers as well as your Associates.** Make sure that you are keeping your customers in the crosshairs, particularly if the issue is affecting them directly. Make sure that those above you are completely aware of the impact of the crisis. Now is not the time to hide the truth or attempt to insulate those

above you from a clear view of the magnitude of your issues. Do not protect yourself or your people, a crisis is a noteworthy event, and you can bet that others within your organization will find out. You can get in more trouble for a cover-up than the actual transgression. Ask Richard Nixon.

7. **Be aggressive in your effort to seek a solution or to bring other resources to bear.** Every organization has its silos, you must bust through these silos during a crisis. If you have to, jump some levels to make sure that those above you (even if they are a layer or two away from you) have a clear understanding of the scale of the crisis. Make sure your assessment of the severity is accurate. You do not want to be the little boy who cried wolf.

8. **Keep them focused.** Do not let the crisis distract you or your team from your customers. I was in a situation wherein hundreds of my Associates were not getting paid on time or the correct amounts. In some cases, these hard-working people received nothing on payday. Friday was the worst day of the week. I have been asked on more than one occasion from justifiably angry Associates, "How can you tell us to take care of our Customers when you cannot take care of us?" I responded, "If I do not make every attempt to continue to take care of our customers, we will have even bigger problems, once this payroll issue is resolved". This is not to say you need to act like the problem creating the crisis, does not exist. Appearing to ignore its existence is one of the worst things you can do. You do however need to do two things at once. Focus on the crisis as well as normal day-to-day activity or your execution plan. Focus away from the crisis can act as a useful distraction in some cases.

9. **Admit your shortcomings or failures or those of your organization.** If you or others screwed up, admit it. It is not necessary to name names, however, if your problems were caused by internal errors, you can admit and defend them at the same time, unless of course, the mistakes were intentional. Show some empathy. If your Customers or Associates are angry and exhibiting what appears to be resentment towards you or your

team, make every effort not to take it personally. Understand that they have a right to be angry. Chances are you have some of the same feelings within you about the situation but must stay calm, cool, and collected. If you have built up even an ounce of trust, rest assured they are mad at the circumstances and not you.

10. **Be firm, in charge, and decisive while understanding some people will crack.** Everyone has a breaking point. Be on the lookout for those who might be about to go over the edge. Check-in with them and try to nurture them without babying them.

11. **Do a post-mortem, or after-action report, to maximize learning and prevent a repeat of the same mistake.** Chances are you will have a clearer perspective once you are on the other side of the calamity and can use hindsight. Pragmatic unemotional analysis is far easier at this point. Start from the beginning with your autopsy. What was the first thing that went wrong?

   • What existed in your company/organization that allowed this issue to expand into a crisis?

   • What have you changed to ensure this problem does not happen again? Make an attempt to quantify the damage.

   • Which customers were hurt or lost, and what can be done to repair the relationship?

   • Recognize those who stepped up to help you out of the quagmire and determine if any formal follow-up is in order for those within your organization that may have caused the problem.

   • Use this time to make sure your organization has gotten past the crisis and prevent them from living in the past. There will be some within your group that will want to wallow in the drama for many days, weeks to come. You need to help them get past it and not allow them to use this unfortunate event for some sort of post-traumatic stress excuse for underperforming. Remind them that it's over, a few times, and then stop talking about the crisis and simply get back to executing your plans.

You may have noticed a theme within these tips! Be proactive. The crisis is the priority. It is not the only priority as mentioned, however, this is an instance where you will want to error on the side of action versus inaction. Remember, we are defined by those instances that challenge us the most. This is your opportunity for growth.

As a leader your actions are always closely watched. During a crisis, you are under a microscope and the stakes have gone up. Welcome to Leadership. To some extent, I always felt that new Managers were rookies until they had successfully completed their first bonified crisis. Similar to any initiation you should look forward to it with mixed emotions but know that it is part of the process. You probably were able to experience a crisis when you were not in a position of Leadership. Let's hope you behaved so that your Karma is in good shape for the inevitable.

And for those of you who have been through this already, I am sure you understand how valuable the past and future lessons will be.

CHAPTER FIVE

CURIOSITY –
WHY IT IS SO IMPORTANT

Curiosity is one of the key components necessary for success as a Leader. I have found that it is an attribute that is a leading indicator of one's ability to be creative. For some reason, those who are curious, seem to also maintain a high level of creativity. Curiosity can lead to many positive traits that I will discuss briefly in this chapter.

Of course, all the great inventors in our history had a high concentration of curiosity. In fact, it may have been their predominant trait. I would venture to guess that our Business Leaders possess a similar level of curiosity as well. They have a drive to "figure it out" and a need for understanding, which has as its basis an inquisitive disposition.

A Curious Manager will have a big appetite for learning. They won't accept the "Because that's the way we have always done it" justification.

For some reason, it is easier for them to relate to customers and accurately predict their reactions to various commercial ideas.

They are very often exceptional listeners who lean toward a literal interpretation of written or spoken words. We once had a slogan that we were force-feeding to our associates which were… "Give our customers, what they want, when they want it". This was a home delivery business that visited the customer once every two weeks. The Curious Manager questioned this slogan by pointing out the following. "If we are supposed to be giving our customers what they want when they want it, why do we give them an annual delivery calendar telling them what day we will deliver?"

When I was hiring Managers, I looked for this attribute in candidates that I was considering bringing into the organization or promoting from within the Company. If you are unable to determine a candidate's level of curiosity during the interview process, you can attempt to determine one's level by examining their creativity. It's been my experience that the two competencies are normally connected. On occasion, I would conclude an interview with a request to send me three questions by tomorrow morning that you think I can answer. I had no intention of answering the questions. I simply wanted to see where their mind went with this opportunity. The curious will ask big picture questions. The non-curious will be focused on issues that concern themselves and not the Company that they are attempting to work at.

There are times when you may observe the antithesis of curiosity in one of your Associates. I think we have all been exposed to the Manager who simply exists. They survive by being good at simply getting the laundry out. In other words, they maintain the situation. They will not typically improve the result. However, they will execute other tactics and strategies and, in some cases, they will do it very well. While there may be a role for them within your organization, their lack of curiosity can hinder them and may limit their upward mobility.

When you think about it, curiosity is one of the first emotions that we attempt to articulate. Our very first questions are often laced with curiosity when as a child we incessantly ask Why? Why? Why? It has been my observation that this curiosity leads to a discovery of facts and conditions that will contribute to a creative solution.

When we ask questions, it is our need to know, that we are attempting to satiate. In business, this need to know is the ground floor to our efforts to solve a problem. Curiosity will give us the information we need to proceed with our decision-making process. If we lack curiosity, we are more apt to proceed without enough facts.

Curious people ask a lot of questions as they are attempting to study a problem from many different angles and enjoy promoting an unorthodox opinion. They are thinkers and typically ponder their next move before making it. You can bet they are well informed on the subject matter and have uncovered data or massaged the information in such a way that clarity is added into the equation.

Curious people tend to consider all the possibilities, or at least most of them. When they look at an issue, they are attempting to reverse engineer the issue or perform a dissection in their attempt to fully understand the problem and improve upon the process. The interesting part is that they often do not even realize they are doing it.

I believe that curious people generally consider the human impact of their decisions. They are interested in the emotions of both customers and employees as they seek to understand the nature of the opportunity they are faced with.

Curious people are not afraid of disagreeing or challenging conventional thought. If they are respectful in their disagreement or challenges, this should not create difficulty, because their point of view will often be the right path. In my opinion, you want people on your team that will challenge you. You will not as a group, get to the best course of action, without some disagreement along the way. If it is coming from your curious and creative co-workers, you should embrace the content of their point of view and consider it closely.

Yes, people with a high degree of curiosity tend to question and even challenge conventional thought. Don't mistake the Manager who overuses the freedom to challenge with the Manager who has a high degree of curiosity. The curious have a goal of improving the situation, the bad one simply likes to point out what's wrong in the world. How to determine the difference? The curious Manager will provide alternative plans after gathering information.

While many attributes are innate and, in some cases, cannot be taught, curiosity is one that can be developed. It takes some time; however, I have seen those that were simply task-oriented develop an attitude that included questioning, researching, and gathering opinions with a focus on both the root cause of a problem as well as a creative solution.

CHAPTER SIX

TIPS FOR A NEWLY PROMOTED FRONT LINE MANAGER

This chapter is intended for those people who are promoted for the first time into a Leadership position. Those selected into this type of assignment, are typically promoted from within an organization and in many cases are put into a position to lead their former peers.

The contents of this chapter represent one of my first attempts to document my opinions on Management. I was sharing my experiences with someone many years ago and was told that I should put my thoughts down on paper so that they could be shared and remembered. I eventually followed up and from time to time I would share these thoughts when I felt I had a receptive audience.

On one occasion I gave it to a first-time Manager shortly before I left the Region in which this individual and I worked. We subsequently lost touch over the years. 10 years later he contacted me to thank me for the advice. He showed me the original document that I had given him and told me that he had passed it onto others. So, if nothing else, sharing my point of view had a positive impact on another person, and thereby provided me the motivation to finish this composition.

It has been my observation that one in three fails in the near term and two of three fail over the long term. The near-term failures either step down or are asked to step down or leave the organization by those who promoted them. The long-term failures are slightly different, as they manage to do just enough not to get terminated. They will languish for many years and almost go unnoticed as a result of their effort to simply survive. They are not to be mistaken for the Sergeants within an organization. Sergeants do not desire promotion and take great satisfaction out of leading Front- Line Associates. They identify with them and understand them. They never forget their roots and are a vital part of the operation. They provide stability, a sense of calm during a crisis and are the keys to communication up to and down the chain.

The following tips if adhered to can allow a new Manager to succeed in the first year when most of the Leaders mistakes are made. It can provide the foundation for a solid career and allow for more rapid development of skills in the years to come.

1.   **Get to know your people quickly.** The best place to do this is in their office not in yours. The office may, in many cases, mean their environment. While not every employee has an office/cubicle most have a workstation, truck, or location where they work with your customers. Make every attempt to place yourself into this environment remembering it is their environment. Do a lot of watching at first and focus on listening. Find a way not to be a desk jockey, do not hide in your new office. Observe both their work habits and what appears to motivate and or de-motivate them.

2.   **Approach your job as a Leader with the goal of removing obstacles for your people.** Serve them and they will serve you.

3.   **Don't do their job for them but show them how to do their job better.** If they need you to answer every question for the rest of their career and don't learn along the way, they will not develop the skills necessary to be successful. Create a learning environment. It is highly likely that they know more about how to do their job than you do. Do not be afraid to admit that and seek help in learning from your staff. Very often they know what is wrong and how to fix it yet lack the influence or access that you may have that is necessary to effect change. Give them credit for the ideas you take and follow-up on. More ideas will come your way as a result.

4. **Never forget that you are their Manager.** Some will try to get you in a position where your role could be compromised. You can and should socialize with them, however, always remember you are the boss.

5. **Create high expectations – your Team will only achieve what you believe they "can" achieve.** Articulate your expectations and consistently repeat your convictions about how and why goals need to be achieved.

6. **Understand that there are two ways to gain respect.** Demanding it and earning it. Demanding it will often cause it to fade away, earning it will last forever. You earn it through demonstrating ethics, service, understanding, and setting the example.

7. **You should seldom take them all on at once.** Change management sometimes demands that we take on the whole group, however, whenever possible, do everything you can to limit the number of people you are "fighting with".

8. **Recognize achievement or "catch them doing something right".** We cannot look at the world through rose-colored glasses, however, it is our nature and the nature of our people to often look for the negative in a situation. Most employees spend most of their day doing it right. The minimal number of mistakes, gets a lot of attention. Make sure you are taking a balanced approach to feedback. Don't forget to recognize your own achievement. Leadership at times can feel lonely and thankless. You need to always keep your eye on the future. However, you should periodically take inventory of what you have developed with your team and yourself.

9. **Rely on your peers, your Supervisor, and whoever else you consider a confidant.** Don't be afraid to admit you do not know. You are in the enviable honeymoon period. Take advantage of the fact that most of your people will understand that you have a lot to learn. Try to find someone to mentor you. This can be someone within your organization or outside of it.

10. **Always seek personal improvement and learning.** Practical experience or on-the-job training through trial and error cannot be discounted, yet we all need to augment our growth through self-study and awareness of both the business and the human condition.

It is recommended that these tips are reviewed periodically. They will not be memorized nor executed effectively, simply by reading them once. Keep them handy and review, review, review.

CHAPTER SEVEN

VISIBILITY

The need to be viewed as visible is far more important in today's world than it was twenty or thirty years ago. It was easier way back when, to rule from the Ivory Tower, even if your Tower was not very tall.

As the business world strives for ever-increasing levels of efficiency and productivity, there has been almost constant pressure to increase one's span of control and or a number of direct and consequently indirect reports.

At the same time, the technology related to the information age provides methods for communications that contain attributes that can be both good and bad. Productive and destructive. Create clarity and confusion and create a need for more and more communication.

Visibility is often accomplished virtually and often on a mass scale. Large conference calls either audio-only or with video allows us to be in many places at once and are without a doubt valuable. They also make the rare opportunity to interact face-to-face more important than ever. Maximize the quality of that time since it is difficult in this era to increase the quantity.

Putting a human personal touch to communication seems to be headed towards obsolescence. Therefore, those that endeavor to overcome this cultural phenomenon will have a leg up on those who allow this trend to affect their approach.

Being visible allows you to practice all the components of the communication model to include listening, reading body language, exhibiting body language and most importantly showing your audience that you are human. Those a layer or two or more away from you will acquire a series of emotions towards you that can be counterproductive, such as fear, suspicion, resentment, and general lack of trust.

Being visible can be difficult on many levels, not least of which is finding the time. You also will be putting yourself in a position to receive feedback that may contain some very difficult questions. While it is easy to pause when answering a question via email or even the phone. A pause in front of a live person or persons can result in further distrust, the creation of a mob mentality, and the general circling of the drain. In short, your well-intentioned efforts can backfire.

The keys to being visible need not be mistaken with the keys to good communication. Those tips are covered in other chapters of this book.

The keys are simple...

1. **Make it a habit and part of virtually every day.** If you miss a day, attempt to make up for it the following day by being visible to more people or workgroups. In fact, if your responsibilities result in limiting your visibility, it becomes even more important for you to be visible. Particularly if you have been away at a "meeting". Left to their own devices, people tend to jump to conclusions that are far more destructive than the truth.

2. **Make sure your visibility includes a combination of formal and informal meetings.** Formal would be situations where you are speaking to groups and presenting your point of view. While there may be a forum included in this effort for receiving questions, if you are doing most of the talking, the effort falls into the formal category. One-on-one meetings or meetings where you are primarily listening to questions fall into the informal category.

3. **The higher you go in the organization the more important it is for you to pre-announce your arrival.** While every level should periodically "pop-in", giving ample warning will set the right mood. Like it or not, when a mid-level or upper Manager pops in, it is viewed by those at lower levels as an attempt to

"catch" employees doing something wrong. This may prevent the free flow of information and will tend to "formalize" what might otherwise be an opportunity for some good dialogue.

4. **Be prepared and have a message.** Make every attempt to get some sort of message across. This can be in the form of group or individual recognition, sponsorship of a company initiative, and or the Companies vision and strategy. Your people want you to have the answers. Even if they do not agree with you, they want to feel that their Leadership is in charge and has a plan.

5. **Get comfortable.** Spend some time doing their job, place yourself in their environment.

6. **If you hear something that is worthy of follow-up, do that!** Follow-up and make sure that the person or persons understand their concern was followed upon.

7. **Listen, listen, listen.** Take notes or ask that someone records issues for you. Your level of execution in terms of follow-up and follow-through is being watched very closely.

8. **Being visible in front of small, medium and large groups increases your visibility efficiency, however, there is nothing like one-on-one connections.** Make every attempt to have a mixture. You will notice two components of face-to-face meetings. 1) People are more polite alone than they are with a group. Limits grandstanding 2) People will be more open if you allow them to be.

9. **Be present.** You may only spend seconds with a person, do your best to avoid all distractions for those seconds. Make eye contact! Listen attentively. Fight the urge to answer or look at your phone. Make that person feel important! If you do not have time for a conversation at least wave, smile, and recognize your fellow human beings. After all, they are important and the reason you are needed.

10. **Make every effort to keep the door to your office open.** Closed doors can make people feel like something is wrong? What can

be occurring that requires privacy?

11. **Park in a different spot every day.** I am not a fan of assigned parking spots. If you have the freedom, move your parking around. The further from the office the better (of course within reason). In one of the locations I managed, there was an assigned place for me to use right next to the office. I chose to park across the street with everyone else. One day on my walk into the office an employee joined me and we chatted along the way. As we walked up to the office, he asked me "why do you park over with us instead of close to the building? I said, "if I did that, I would not have had the chance to chat with you for 2 minutes today, and besides I need the exercise."

12. **Break up your patterns on occasion.** Do not do it on a regular basis but on occasion, you're wandering around should be a surprise and at odd hours. You will see some stuff that will help you improve your performance. At some point in your career, you are going to work for that person who has a knack for showing up at the worst possible time. Those Managers are not simply lucky! They in fact are disciplined and have this knack because they wander around more than others.

13. **You are bound to run into someone who is having a problem with a company policy or how said policy or strategy was communicated.** Put another way, they will attempt to get their boss in trouble. This usually starts with "Can I say something off the record?" My answer to that is always "Well that depends. If you tell me something that must be followed up on, I may need to divulge the source of my knowledge. I will do my best to avoid that but cannot promise it". Depending on the severity of the issue, it is best to focus on listening and not talking. If you do talk, most of what comes out of your mouth should be questions intended to clarify. You might be able to solve something via quick clarification to include justification for the decision that is causing concern. One of your follow-up questions might be "What is it that you are hoping to get out of our discussion?" Be careful about commitments at this point. If follow-up is necessary, then be sure to do so.

14. **Try whenever you can to do it alone.** When you are part of an entourage it has a buffering effect and reduces the comfort level of those you are attempting to be visible with.

15. **Quick Pointers –**

    a. Get your own coffee on occasion if someone normally gets it for you.

    b. Same with using the copier.

    c. Try to take someone to lunch that you might not otherwise interact with.

    d. If you have a need to go on a road trip or tour, take someone with you. There is nothing like an automobile to relax someone and even create memories.

    e. Have others teach you their job. Even if for only a few minutes. You will learn about the obstacles they face and the reasons they are successful. And they will likely never forget the interaction.

This will all take discipline and will seem like it's going great until one day you wake up and realize you have essentially quarantined yourself because you were too busy. You will know you have it right when two things occur. You enjoy it when you're doing it and miss it when you stop doing it.

CHAPTER EIGHT

BUILDING TRUST

I hesitated to include this topic in the book as it is difficult to explain the process of building trust while making every effort to be concise.

The ability to build trust or create an environment is more of an attribute than skill in my opinion. In many or most cases, the untrustworthy cannot be taught to be trustworthy. While a trustworthy person can indeed be corrupted.

As with most attributes or personality components, there is both a good and bad side to trust. At its core, trust includes consistency. Therefore, even evil people can build trust. Many of history's more evil Leaders were "consistently" evil and could be trusted to act in a certain way. Hitler gained the trust of millions and while most would agree that those closest to him were pure evil, many of the masses that followed him were essentially good people at least before Hitler came along. Depending on your perspective, they were either duped, brainwashed, or simply plain ignorant. The point being, Hitler indeed built a certain level of trust. The sentiment obviously did not endure and ultimately most people saw him for what he really was.

Walter Cronkite, who was labeled the most trusted man in America attained this moniker via **consistency** as well as **honesty**. Those are the two primary execution points necessary for building trust followed by **selflessness** and **caring**. I will therefore expand on those four attributes as I attempt to explain the keys to building trust.

1. **Consistency** – As a Leader you are consistently under a microscope. Your words and actions are watched more closely than you may realize. Much like we track the statements and positions

of our Politicians. Those both above you and below you will adjust their assessment of your trustworthiness based upon your level of consistency. The Manager who adjusts his/her point of view on a situational basis to please a Direct Report, Peer, Boss, or other higher-ranking Manager will soon be discovered as someone who cannot be trusted. This does not mean that they will quickly fail as you will read in the chapter on "being a Suckboy" however it will not endear them to those they work with and ultimately limit their effectiveness. To do this, rely on your personal convictions. If your default position is your belief system, it will be easier for you to practice consistency. As we mature and experience more life, our values are bound to change. What may follow is a change in the opinion which could be viewed as inconsistent behavior. As a result, you must take the necessary time to explain your changing perspective, particularly when it comes to those issues that you have been most vociferous about.

2. **Honesty** – Webster's indicates that honesty must include truthfulness and sincerity. If you dig deeper and define truthfulness, you will find that honesty must correspond with fact or reality, while sincerity has at its base "good faith". To distill this down into one singular piece of advice, "tell the truth". Seems simple, however, it is like golf. You can improve, yet nobody has ever perfected it. Very few can get through a day without exhibiting some form of dishonesty such as withholding facts, shading the truth, telling a white lie, not letting the facts get in the way of a good story, and putting a "spin" on something. In fact, these terms were invented to take some of the sting out of a statement being labeled as dishonest or worse yet a lie. Similar to golf, honesty is something you must consciously practice if you are going to improve. It obviously goes hand in hand with consistency and will be noticed over time versus one of those attributes that is immediately recognized.

3. **Selflessness** – You will build trust if you approach your position of leadership with a selfless attitude. If you believe one of your primary roles is to remove obstacles for your people, whether they be internal or external, you will build trust. Think of your own

experience with people you have worked for. They will exhibit three categories of behavior. A remover of obstacles, a creator of obstacles, or one who has no effect on obstacles. Which type of Leader would you want to work for? Compare the motivation of working for someone who is an asset to your roles and responsibilities as an employee versus one who consistently blocks your progress.

4. **Caring** – If you exhibit genuine caring towards your fellow co-workers despite their standing in the organization, you will build trust. This trust will not be limited to those who benefit from your kind gestures or actions but will be viewed favorably by others. Again, your every action is being watched very closely. The emphasis on being genuine cannot be understated. If your caring is in fact, disingenuous, your efforts will have the opposite effect as you will be viewed as shallow, manipulative, and deceitful.

Some components of building a trusting environment include the following actions.

1. **Favoritism is an instant trust killer.** We are always going to have certain members of our staff that we are more aligned with than others. You must work very hard to avoid showing favoritism to these folks. If you have a long-term relationship with a staff member, even if it is pure, you will be accused of favoritism. Be aware of that! Often you might have to be tougher on those that are closer to you. You can justify it to them by explaining that you feel comfortable pushing them harder because you know their capabilities. It is best to self-police yourself with what might be perceived as the favorite(s). Be mindful of how your relationship with others is perceived.

2. **Be willing to change your mind.** Leaders must be decisive and have conviction about their point of view. However, if you go great lengths of time without changing your outlook or position on any point of debate, you can be assured that this is a warning sign that your view of work and life is narrowing. Sincerely examine and consider the viewpoint of others. Admitting a mistake or even

adjusting your point of view is a powerful method of gaining trust. Of course, you must believe in this new way of doing something, don't simply change your mind to build trust. That insincere act will do more damage than good.

3. **Give credit to others.** You should be a cheerleader for your team. This is not always possible and is an easily forgotten task. Again, it must be sincere, or it will be viewed as pandering. Nobody likes a braggart, however, if you're complimenting the achievements of others it makes you both look good. You don't want to turn work into a love fest so don't be over-emotional about it and for sure, try to apply it evenly with a combination of group recognition of achievement as well as individual. Some of it is public, some of it semi-public and some of it private.

Typically, the leader that embodies a trustworthy personality has a firm handle on what his/her beliefs and values are. They know who they are and have a keen view of their own strengths and weaknesses. They are humble, yet confident. Their confidence does not display itself in such a way that they are viewed as egomaniacs or narcissistic. When examined closely, these untrustworthy people are viewed as insecure. Their twisted efforts to soothe their own insecurities result in them creating an environment where trust is superficial at best. The longer you know them, the less you trust them.

To build an environment of trust, one must believe in the importance of trust. Think of all the things we have that we either trust or distrust…

*   Spouse

*   Children

*   Friends

*   Boss

*   Teacher

*   Coworker

- Police

- Doctors

- Airline Pilot

- Government

The list is endless, and we all fall into a point of view that is somewhere between "everything and everyone in this world are trying to harm me, including those dogs barking all the time" and "Everything is going to be just perfect, nothing is ever going to go wrong".

It all starts with a personal belief. There are many that do not value trust. Their reasons may in fact be valid or somewhat valid. In considering how you want to approach the issue of trust you must first look inward. If it is important to you, that is to say, you want to trust and be trusted, then you are likely to refine your style and approach to match that personal belief.

We are all a work in progress when it comes to our own personal performance in the area of trust. My goal in this regard is to make every attempt to be more trusting and trusted next year, than I was last year. What's yours?

CHAPTER NINE

SURFACING RESISTANCE

It is vitally important that you remain in touch with the opinions and feelings of those you are responsible for leading. It helps you to identify where they are at, in terms of the change cycle and will help you determine where you need to go with your communication. Surfacing resistance can be a frightening endeavor and you need to gird your loins for what you are going to hear.

While it may seem counterintuitive, there are some huge benefits to surfacing resistance.

So why surface resistance? It is a simple answer. If it exists, you want to know about it so you can do something about it. As a result, you and your organization will be more effective.

In most cases, you cannot address those issues that you do not know about. As is typically the case, ignorance is not bliss when it comes to Leadership. You have a responsibility to know how the troops are feeling.

Make no mistake, you are not paid, to simply keep them happy, however, if you can avoid upheaval or better yet build trust and a better environment, through providing more information or allowing people a forum to air their feelings, you will be a more effective leader.

If you attempt to surface it and find nothing, do not become overconfident, it may still exist, they are just not telling you, for some reason.

If you do not surface resistance, it will remain underground and could fester. Even if it is a relatively small item, many small things typically turn into one big thing.

Typical initial reactions to this topic are...

- I don't need to surface resistance, my people are already willing to tell me what they are unhappy about!

- If you ask them to complain, they will!

- Why on earth would I want to do that, things are going great right now!

- I don't care if they don't like it, as it won't make a difference in how we move forward. (If this is your belief, you may have wasted your money on this book)

Even if you surface resistance the right way, you could trigger reactions that create a certain amount of risk. If you have built up trust, you should expect frank criticism of the topic you are attempting to surface resistance on. How you react to this criticism, which could be directed at either you or your organization is one of the keys to using this method for improvement in both your results and the environment/ culture you are attempting to create/change.

The basic approaches to surfacing resistance are as follows...

1. **There are instances, where you may want to attempt to surface resistance in advance of the announcement of a change.** Taking one or two Associates aside in advance can create a higher level of trust and may help you not only surface resistance but overcome it. They will undoubtedly (if you pick the right ones) tell you what and why in terms of where the resistance will come from. They may even tell you the "Who". Consider your conversations as "practice". You might get some feedback that will help you with the broader communication and there is even the chance that you might create allies. This is not an attempt to divide and conquer, to the contrary, the tactic has the goal of building a coalition and prepare you for broader communication.

2. **Separately or in conjunction with the previous step, make an attempt to get to the influencers within the group in advance.** This surfacing is indeed a divide and conquer tactic. The target(s) of this communication has other monikers such as Leader, Jailhouse Lawyer, Rabble Rousers, Shit Stirrers, Skeptics, Cynics, Doubting Thomas and Pessimists to name a few. Despite these ugly labels, they are not necessarily a bad thing. In fact, they very often are loyal to the organization. You will find that in times of major change, even if people do not believe in them, they can garner temporary or long-term followers. Good to know them and keep them close. They might even cause you to modify the message. Typically, they are more than willing to resist. It's already on the surface with them.

3. **If you run into a shit-stirrer there are times when you need to back them down.** Don't do this the first few times they resist. Try to examine their motive and determine if the concern is genuine. And it is usually better to do it in private, however, sometimes it must be public. Many years ago, during a cost-cutting season, it was decided to eliminate the company picnic for one year. There was some unhappiness as this was a nice family event however most understood the urgency due to the economy and the Company's performance. There was a guy in one of my 7 locations that were very vocal about the cancellation. Long after the event would have occurred, he would voice his strong disagreement with this decision, and it was always in a crowd of people. To show his courage he again challenged me publicly on my decision. I explained the rationale one more time, however this time I concluded it by asking him if he had gone to last year's picnic. (I knew the answer) He said no. I then said did you go to the picnic 2 years ago? No? Three years ago? No. The fact is he had never attended a company picnic. He stopped being the self-appointed spokesman for the "People who are angry about the picnic be canceled, who have never gone" committee.

4. **Remember that one on one can occur before or after a critical announcement is almost always more effective.** While the initial effort to surface resistance cannot always be attempted in

advance it can in follow-up. A simple "So what did you think of our announcement? should elicit some feedback.

5. **If you are in a group setting, guard against the self-anointed spokesperson high jacking your message in front of the group, they may or may not represent the consensus of the group.** Work to involve a cross-section of people into the discussion. To get others involved in the discussion you might choose to say something like "Dave you have been good at sharing your opinion, which I appreciate, now let's hear from some other people who are present here today.

6. **If you are a mid-level Manager and have Managers that report to you, make every effort to determine the point of view of all your staff.** The more potentially volatile the issue, the more you need to do in terms of sense. You won't always be aligned, however, when you're not, it is better if you know that than if you don't.

7. **Seek outside help on determining the pulse of your organization.** Not every day or every month, however, it can occur every year or every other year. While this can be expensive, it may be the best method if you happen to believe your people will not talk to you for some reason. There is another chapter in the book that delves into this tactic further titles Third-party listening posts.

Keep these seven guiding principles in mind as you embark on your efforts to surface resistance…

1. **Make every attempt to not take the criticism personally.** Remain pragmatic and find some comfort in the fact that your people are talking to you, rather than someone else. Their complaints are a natural part of the process and will help you and your company get better.

2. **Listen – Listen – Listen.** Pace your response, contemplate your answers and seek to find common ground on this issue. It is almost equally important that your folks feel they have been heard, versus feeling that you agree with them. If you fire back at them, they will not believe you are listening, even if you are.

3. **Ask them for their solutions.** Ask… What can we do to make this work? Or How would you do this differently? You may find that none of their ideas will work or that you are not able to influence this type of adjustment, but you might learn something that can work, and that will be a home run for you. Don't forget to give them the credit.

4. **Know your stuff.** Be well-read on the subject matter if you intend to have a verbal ping pong match with them. Their resistance more often than not, is simply a result of them not understanding all of the facts related to the change, or the need for the change. Hopefully, you are aligned with your Leadership. If this change is one that you invented and implemented, you should have conviction about it and this conviction should be based upon a compelling argument that you are able to articulate.

5. **Do not pass the buck.** You are paid to represent your Companies point of view. You must be careful about publicly disagreeing with those above you. There may be some exceptions to this rule but be careful. Make sure you understand the party line on why the change is occurring. You may need to do some homework with your own Leadership in advance of your formalized effort to surface resistance.

6. **If you find that you have made a mistake, admit it.** If you are able to take their feedback and modify or adjust your decision, do so and let them know that you listened. Let them know this more than once! Drive home the point that you want their feedback and will on occasion be able to effect change because of their ideas. This will ensure ongoing and healthy two-way communication.

7. **If you make a commitment to get back to them, or follow up on an item, make sure that you do just that.** It will help your credibility and build trust.

Resistance is something you will face in varying degrees throughout your career so you might as well embrace this natural occurrence and work to find some benefit to it. Of course, you will want to always gauge the root cause of the resistance. While resistance is somewhat of a constant, if you are not eventually finding some level of cooperation and buy-in from those who are in your organization, you are in for a long haul in terms of realizing incremental and sustained improvement in your results as well as the culture you are trying to create.

Surfacing it and effectively dealing with it is a powerful skillset that you will find extremely rewarding over time. If you are viewed as someone who listens and gets things done, you will gain loyalty and all the benefits that go along with having that type of reputation.

CHAPTER TEN

EMAIL TIPS

It may seem foolish to include a chapter on something that should be relatively simple. This particular business tool has been somewhat ignored when it comes to suggesting dos and don'ts. The fact that it is easier to list the "don'ts" is indicative of how widespread the abuse is.

When you consider the fact that more than half of the words exchanged in this day and age are done so electronically, it is clear to see some ground rules should be established. It is not good enough to simply understand the many features and tricks that an email software such as Outlook can provide. To that end, the following is a list of the Authors beliefs on the act of emailing.

1. **Determining if you should have a salutation is based upon the business culture and your familiarity with the recipient.** In the U.S., it is usually <u>not necessary</u> to start with a Dear Robert or Hi Robert. It normally won't offend anyone. In many parts of the rest of the world, the lack of a greeting would be considered rude. In the Middle East, I had a staff member tell me that he was offended by his Canadian boss's lack of a greeting as impolite. You should almost always error on the side of being too polite versus too friendly.

2. **Do not be that person who is known as the one who circulates a lot of non-work-related emails.** Whether they be jokes, video clips, or pictures of your vacation to Wally World. Those that do too much of this, are ultimately viewed as nonproductive. Even if people like the jokes.

3. **Avoid Spamsturbation, which are simply, those emails that are unnecessary.** For instance, we all know someone who answers every email with a "Thank you". They are also closely aligned with those that answer every thank you with a "You're Welcome". These habits work to water down true expressions of appreciation. There is nothing wrong with expressing appreciation, however, it should have substance behind it and often be accompanied by more than two words. And do not overdo it or it will become meaningless to the intended recipients.

4. **Don't mass-market your thoughts.** Take extra effort to ensure that everyone addressed, copied, or blind copied on an email will be interested in the content, or will benefit at least a little bit. Violation of this principle seems to happen more often on the last day of work for some people, as they say, farewell to all 8,000 email users and good friends that they made during their 4 months with the company.

5. **Beware of the usage of the BCC (Blind Carbon Copy) line.** The author learned this lesson the hard way when his BCC addressee, replied to all, therefore alerting the targeted addressee (and a few others) that another party was secretly brought into the discussion as an observer. If you really find it necessary to provide someone else with a surreptitious copy, simply resend your sent message to the person you would otherwise copy.

6. **Be careful in what you forward.** One of the more common mistakes made in this regard is the practice of forwarding one of your Boss's emails that admonish you to improve in a certain area. This is de facto passing of the buck and can contribute to self-marginalizing your position with both your Team and your Managers. The Manager that forwards his Bosses email with cryptic commentary such as "He makes a good point here", "What are we going to do about this?", " I could not have said it better myself" is exhibiting a variety of traits that hurt his/her effectiveness. Beyond being viewed as someone who is simply a puppet for their boss, they could be or are viewed as someone who will not contribute to the dialogue necessary to improve.

They could be viewed as lazy and lacking in terms of vision and creativity. So, yes! Be very careful.

7. **Work very hard at brevity.** Like the format of this book, long emails are not read with the same amount of attention as short ones are. If you gain a reputation as being long-winded, there is an increased likelihood that your emails will not even get opened. If they are opened, they may only get scanned. Approach most emails as a summary of the message. If further instruction is needed, place it on an attachment.

8. **You can effectively bring attention to segments of your message via bolding, underlining, changing the color or font size, however, guard against overuse of this and do not use it before effectively practicing the advice in item number 5.** If you use this tactic and your email begins to look like a ransom note created from cutting out letters from a magazine and pasting them on an A 5, it is a sign you have overdone it.

While email is one of our most useful tools for communicating, it has contributed to environmental changes that can inhibit the communication process. In extreme cases, it has provided instances where termination for cause was necessary as a result of an email faux pau.

Because the use of emails has become so pervasive, it is worthwhile to list a few of the land mines created by the increased usage of email.

• Discoverable emails have provided a windfall for Plaintiffs' attorneys. Attorneys love the treasure trove of evidence that can be mined from a litigation hold on all emails. As such, try your best to avoid sending a message that you would not want an attorney to discover. Better to go to a payphone like in the old days.

• As we all strive to be more and more efficient, we can find ourselves at a point where email is close to being our "only" communication device, limiting face-to-face contact and all the benefits of a live conversation. Neither voice inflection, nor body language can translate over an email. Fortunately, Skype, Facetime, and Zoom have come along to help offset this phenomenon.

- It can be one of the primary factors in disturbing the work – home life balance. We can either become a victim or victimize others via the twenty-four hour daily barrage of emails. Some of us may have worked for the Manager who enjoys plastering us with a series of nasty grams on a Sunday afternoon, effectively shortening our weekend and the weekend of our families. Working seven days a week, can at times be necessary, however more often than not, it can be avoided. You may not be able to control inbound emails and the timing; however, you can be careful not to mimic bad behavior.

- E-mail correspondence is not a grammar-free zone! Utilize your spell check and be mindful of your sentence structure. For those of us who are particularly challenged in this area, we should get into the practice of double-checking our work. If the E-mail is going to or has a remote chance of going to anyone more than one level above you, you may choose to double-check. If you happen to be unable to "see" your errors, try reading the email out loud to yourself. Sometimes our hearing is much better than our site. The exception to this rule, is e-mails typed from a handheld device. We should of course do our best; however fat finger syndrome allows for a higher error rate in my opinion.

The ability to communicate in writing is a critical component of a Leader's toolbox. Your particular level of expertise will be exposed to many, many people. And it will not only be your intended audience that views the good, the bad, and the ugly when it comes to your style of writing.

The size of the chapters in this book is a message. It is the small things that count. Little nuances can make a difference. When you aggregate all of the small things, you suddenly have provided the entire portrait. As a Leader, you are subject to an increased level of scrutiny. You are being watched and judged by those above you, at your level, as well as your direct reports. Welcome to Leadership.

CHAPTER ELEVEN

MISTAKES

Inherent in your role as a Manager in the responsibility to make decisions with stakes that are typically greater than they were in your non-Leadership role. It is likely that you will find you are called upon to make decisions more frequently. And they affect others to a greater extent. In short, the stakes are higher.

Averagely, your decisions in the past affected only you and your customers, while now, your decisions affect a wider swath of the organization and likely the customer base. All this leads to more scrutiny of your decision-making. Your decisions will be examined for the timeliness, creativity, as well as impact on the organization and from a financial and or non-financial perspective.

Your actions and decisions will be viewed from more angles now. In the past, it was primarily viewed from above or maybe from your peers as well as customers. As a Leader, your track record will be examined with more granularity from all three of those entities plus by those who are being led by you, your Direct Reports, or Staff.

For most of us, we make very few mistakes as a proportion of all our actions and decisions. Think of your last commute to and from work. You have probably made thousands of decisions without even thinking about them. Possibly there may have been some instances where you made some bigger, high-stakes decisions that either kept you or others safe. And most of the time you get it right.

To continue the comparison, in terms of mistakes using motor vehicles, imagine you were commuting in a big safe SUV, and you are now on a Motorcycle. Your current mode of transportation as a Leader is faster and more fun to drive and you are better off financially (Lower cost for the vehicle, insurance, fuel, and maintenance) however there is a tradeoff. Clearly, it is more dangerous. Mistakes by you have greater consequences, especially for you! Since the speed is increased in your current mode of transportation you need to make decisions faster. Furthermore, there is less forgiveness in terms of mistakes made by the other drivers you are on the road with. Both vehicles can lead to death or injury, but there is a higher incidence of severe injury on a per capita basis as a Leader.

It is important to do some categorization of mistakes. There are many ways to slice up the mistake pie, however, in keeping with this book's objective of an uncomplicated approach, I will distill them into two basic categories.

> **FATAL MISTAKES**   These are mistakes that are an overt disregard for rules or laws. They are the type of decisions that can lead to your termination either immediately or via a progressive discipline process. And severe cases financial and legal consequences

> **ERRORS IN JUDGEMENT** These are everyday run-of-the-mill errors that are by themselves relatively insignificant. However, if there is a higher-than-average rate of this type of mistake your reputation will be impacted. Celebrities/Politicians like to use this "Error in Judgment" label for mistakes that are closer to fatal than they would like you to believe. For a cheating spouse, the mistake was "an error in judgment", while the husband's spouse would likely consider infidelity a "fatal mistake".

Ok, so we have established some perspective on mistakes, now let's cover some salient points that should be remembered as we consider this topic. These guidelines provide sound advice regardless of the type of mistake. Their application may vary in terms of approach or degree of intensity, nonetheless, they provide a foundation for dealing with the many mistakes you are going to make throughout your career.

Learn from your mistake with the intent of **not repeating** your blunders. Our degree of learning from a mistake is often in direct correlation to the amount of pain we incur as a result of our gaffe. We need to develop mechanisms that allow us to learn from all our mistakes instead of just the ones that cause us injury. When you realize you have made a mistake (for some of us, this is the hardest part of the process) take a little time to turn back the clock and do a quick diagnosis of what caused you to go down that path. Ask yourself some quick questions…

- **Did I not have enough knowledge about the subject matter?**

- **Did I not listen to good counsel?**

- **Did I get bad counsel?** Be careful with this one, as you may begin to pass the buck by not answering this one honestly.

- **Was it simply a matter of bad timing?**

- **Were my objectives pure?** A hidden and or selfish agenda has fouled up many Leaders.

- **Did I properly communicate?** Did I make the necessary case for change, and did I listen both prior to and following the implementation of my decision?

- With some or all of these questions answered, finish this sentence "My decision to *fill in the blank was a mistake, however, I learned that I will not fill in the blank* in the future".

Obviously, if you get bogged down in this process, you will make fewer mistakes in the future, simply because you will spend all your time analyzing your past missteps. Over-analysis of anything is a mistake within itself, so you will need to develop skills that allow you to go through these steps in a matter of minutes or in some cases seconds. Make every attempt to apply this process proportionately in relation to the magnitude of the mistake.

- **Do not fear errors in judgment.** You are going to make mistakes! Approaching your job with an over-emphasis on caution and perfection will cause you to be ineffective as you will become paralyzed. Leadership to some extent is about taking risks. Your desire to promote and move up in an organization is risky in itself. If you become the Leader that relies on everyone else to make the tough decisions, you will be viewed simply as a follower. Errors in judgment if repeated often enough, can by virtue of their collective impact morph into a fatal mistake. If you are making enough errors in judgment to place your future in jeopardy, you should be able to see your demise on the horizon. If you are only slightly above average in your mistake rate, you simply risk things like a promotion, merit pay increase, and creditability with those around you. Be smart and keep your motives focused first on the customer, followed by your Associates and your Company. Be unselfish. And be brave.

- **Fear fatal mistakes.** If you have made it into Management, you most certainly have an understanding of what a fatal mistake is. In a sentence, these are the ones that get you fired and fired fast. Another definition is overt disregard for work rules and or laws. The vast majority of Leaders in this world are not fired for fatal mistakes, however, there are always a few. View your evening news and you will periodically be exposed to some great examples of what not to do.

- **Get over it.** Acknowledge the mistake, analyze what caused it, own it, and then move to mitigation. Don't ignore your mistakes, but don't dwell on them for very long. If necessary, compartmentalize the mistake and revisit it later after you have tended to your other priorities.

- **If the mistake affects others, take ownership and apologize if necessary.** You do not need to pay penance for each and every mistake you make. It will take some of that good ole common sense to determine which mistakes actually require you to express regret either publicly or privately. There is immense power in a <u>sincere</u> apology. It is an act that can contribute mightily to building trust. While I did not proceed through my career intent on finding things to apologize for, there were a number of instances where my heartfelt act of contrition resulted in a breakthrough or turning point in a relationship. We are a society of second chances that are granted to those who commit to improvement and take ownership of their actions.

* **Do not attempt to hide your mistakes.** Hopefully, on the bigger decisions, you have provided your Manager with advance notice of your strategies and tactics. There will be times of course where a mistake is made in a vacuum without exposure to those you report to. When it is called for, let your boss know that you have experienced a glitch. Share what went into your thinking and what you have learned from the experience. If possible, explain what you believe the next steps are and get ready to get some feedback. Hopefully, you belong to an organization that supports risk-taking and understands that mistakes will be made. Your best hope for turning this into a positive with those above you is to convince them that this mistake was an investment in your future and the future of the company.

While there may be some information within this chapter that helps you make good decisions in the future via learning from your mistakes, this chapter is not attempting to teach Decision Making. That is another subject worthy of a separate degree of attention.

For me, I have a clear memory of my bigger mistakes. The pain of that experience is easier to remember and connect with than the joy of most accomplishments. I could have written a book about those mistakes.

Buying this book was not a mistake.

CHAPTER TWELVE

YOU WANT TO PROMOTE?
THOUGHTS TO CONSIDER

Assuming that the majority of people who pick up this book are early in their Leadership career this chapter will be helpful to those who are once again considering the next move up. It will help you to understand your motivations as well as preparation for the next step. You may finish the chapter with the opinion that promotion is negative. This could be a byproduct of my effort to point out the many land mines related to the promotion. That decision is up to you.

That is not my goal. I am however making an attempt to help you avoid any missteps along the way. We must have our eyes wide open so that we can accurately assess what is best for us by having full knowledge of the risks. After all, the higher you go in an organization, the higher the mortality rate. One only needs to examine the relatively short life expectancy of our average CEOs to understand the peril. I believe if you consider this advice, it will act to accelerate your efforts to advance by avoiding mistakes.

Believe it or not, there are both good and bad reasons that may be acting to motivate you to promote. Most of them are good, however, it is prudent to have an understanding of some potential stumbling blocks related to your internal desire for another or higher position within your Company or any Company for that matter.

Typically, there will be a variety of emotions that drive you to move up. You could be experiencing a combination of good and bad reasons. In some cases, later in your career, you may find that others are just as motivated for you to promote as you are. Negative motivations when joined with positive motivations are not nearly as bad as when the negative is the primary or stand-alone catalyst for your desire to move up.

Let's get the negative out of the way and discuss some of those "bad" reasons that may be causing you to pursue or at least attempt advancement.

1. **I am applying for the experience of applying alone, I know that I will not get the job and that I am not ready.** – This is a dangerous point of view. If you yourself do not believe you are ready, you can bet that others are in agreement with you. It is likely that this self-doubt, whether it be accurate or not, will reveal itself during the selection process. You risk that the Decision Makers in your Company will arrive at an unfavorable opinion of you as they are exposed to an unprepared candidate. A lack of self-confidence, particularly when it is an accurate opinion is a precarious position to hold as you attempt to advance yourself or even test the waters. It is important to differentiate and diagnose the difference between stretching yourself and simply not being qualified. The only time, when this might be a good idea is when you are unemployed.

2. **I am applying because I do not like my current Job or Manager** – Running away from something or someone is by itself a horrible motivation for promoting. Odds are that if you do not like your current job, it is showing up in your performance. Some people, however, are able to overcome their disdain for their circumstances by using it to motivate them to a higher level of performance. This motivation coupled with enough positive reasons is acceptable, however, as a standalone motivation, you run the risk of going from the frying pan into the fire.

3. **My Peer Promoted and I am envious** – While nobody ever admits this as a reason, Managers are very competitive. I have witnessed perfectly content Managers who have never expressed a desire to promote, nor did they concentrate any effort towards

this goal become instantly discontented when they felt left behind. If you feel this way, look inward first. How you respond to your peers' promotion may validate your decision to grow, a negative reaction can be a misstep. Let some time pass then have a career discussion with your Manager to determine what YOU need to do to position yourself for the next opportunity. If you feel personally attacked or wronged and cannot get over these feelings, it may be time to move on instead of up.

4. **I want to promote because that's what you're supposed to do –** Pursuing promotion based solely upon the expectations of others can be exhausting. I ran into this phenomenon periodically and typically it was driven by two factors. A Spouse/Significant other who had their own motivations related to the power, influence, and wages that are attached to moving up. And from some former members of our Military where Up or Out was the approach used with Officers. It is also employed in some Law firms in terms of becoming a Partner. Again, this reason can be a part of one's desire to promote, it only becomes dangerous when it is the overriding impetus for moving up.

5. **I want to promote so that I can make more money –** While we all need money and it is one of the primary reasons we work, particularly in your early years of employment, money alone or as the main reason can cause you to stumble. There is a risk that you will move into a job that you do not like and or are not suited for as you pursue the almighty buck. I have seen people uproot their family, take a loss on their Real Estate, move away from their family all for a 10% increase in wages. Only to find themselves so unhappy that they ultimately moved back for less pay and ended their chance for advancement for years. Make sure you fully understand the sacrifice! Make every effort to include your loved ones in the decision-making process including informing them of any sacrifices they may need to make. You will want them on your side!

6. **I want to promote for status reasons –** Nobody will ever admit this as their primary reason for wanting to promote, however, we

have all witnessed those individuals who want into what they perceive as "The Club". They are far more image-conscious than most of us. They are the ones that want to promote so badly that it hurts. Like a professional athlete that overcompensates in the effort category, they tend to stumble a lot and miss the free throw when under a lot of pressure.

Be mindful of the career-ending promotion which can be caused by the scenario described in point number 4 above. The career-ending promotion often has the following components attached to it and should prompt some questioning and investigation.

- **Nobody else will take the job** – Do your best to find out why people are not motivated to fill this opening. Is it simply a lack of bench strength? What happened to the last 3 Managers that held that position? These types of situations can actually be turned into an incredibly positive if you survive them.

- **It's a new position that is a test** – Attempt to assess the commitment level of your organization to the test. New positions are seldom labeled as "Test" however one should be clear and attempt to clearly understand both the expectations and the responsibilities of the position. Does the position make sense to you and others? Do you have some of your own ideas that you feel you will be able to implement? Is your company open to risk-taking? What are your organization's stamina when it comes to new ideas?

- **Choose your Boss** – There is no quicker way to end a career than by working for the wrong person. This is not to say that you should avoid a tough Boss. They can often be exactly what is needed. Simply make an attempt to understand who you are working for. This effort can be conducted during the interview process and through a separate investigation. Does the hiring manager have a history of success in his/her field? Do people develop under the tutelage of the hiring Manager? Does the Hiring Manager appear to inspire loyalty? What happened to the person you are replacing?

These three points can be summed up in three words "Understand Your Risks". Since you are already a Manager, you are probably in a better position to make this assessment as you should have access to improved information as well as people within your organization that can help you in this analysis.

In the chapter on Work Ethic, the Peter Principle is briefly explained. Understanding your risk is good preventive medicine that will help you avoid the Peter Principle and ensure that you not only attain the promotion you are pursuing but that you flourish in those positions while preparing yourself for the one after.

Finally, let's talk about some of the positive reasons we might have once we feel we are desirous of a promotion. Note, that these positives by themselves are not typically the only thing you need. You should have many reasons to desire promotion. Here are a few of the good reasons…

1. **I am ready** – I have a consistent level of success in my current position. I have achieved most of my objectives whether they be numerical or in terms of personal development. I have the confidence to again stretch myself and anticipate the challenges as well as look forward to them

2. **Others believe I am ready** – I have received consistent feedback from both those above me and those beside me that I possess the skills necessary for the next level in the organization. In fact, I am being internally pursued and or encouraged to apply for the promotion I am now considering. And or, I have been recruited by those outside of the organization who had actual knowledge of my style and achievements.

3. **I have made a conscious effort to prepare myself for the next level** – I have made an effort to learn whether it be informal or formal. I have continued/completed my education and or gained technical expertise that is necessary for the position I am pursuing. I am a lifelong student of business and have focused on those competencies where I need work. I can articulate a meaningful answer when asked "What have you done to prepare yourself for this position?"

4. **I am either bored or feel I am going to be bored in the near future** – Boredom and how we can deal with it can be harmful to our career. If the stars are aligned, a promotion can take away boredom immediately. You may be wired in such a way that you need greater challenges and influence.

5. **My family and I are aligned** – My promotion will not create a hardship on my family that they are not willing to bear. I have shared my emotional perspective and motivation and we agree that it is the right thing to do at the right time.

6. **I have thoroughly investigated the position and have a vision for how I would proceed** – The promotional opportunity excites me. I have some ideas that I believe I would be the best at implementing. I can visualize myself being successful.

7. **I believe this position is a necessary component of my ultimate plan** – I need and want this experience as it will enhance my opportunity to attain what I believe is my eventual goal.

Determining one's motivation for any important decision takes a heavy dose of emotional integrity. Simply put, are you able to be honest with yourself. A tall task for most of us. It may take some time and patience to determine your true motivation. Our methods for gaining this clarity will vary widely. Some of us must climb a mountain and meditate in solitude to find our career path, others can do it on the daily commute to and from work. Whatever the technique, ensure that you have done your due diligence. It is an important decision.

CHAPTER THIRTEEN

KNOWING WHEN & HOW TO LEAVE "CHANGING EMPLOYERS"

From time to time, throughout your work life, it is likely that you will be faced with a growing desire to do something else, in terms of a career. The cause of these feelings can be driven by either positive or negative events. You may be courted by another employer due to your performance and reputation or you may become dissatisfied by your current environment.

Our feelings in this regard are often driven by the environment. During economic booms, we tend to want to jump on board with the latest Gold Rush and get our slice of the economic expansion which may be facilitated by changing jobs. During an economic downturn and periods of higher unemployment, we tend to be far more grateful for our current situation. It beats the alternative of the unemployed.

Work will not always bring us contentment, however, if it is bringing unhappiness for a prolonged period of time, we should think about changing either our attitude or our job.

Changing jobs can be a risky endeavor particularly if your decision is not well thought out. Over the last 50 years, we have moved away from an environment wherein our predecessors went from school to an employer and then stayed with that Company for 40 or 50 years.

That particular formula is not supported by Company's or their employees in this day and age. Employers have been forced to be less loyal as they respond to changing business conditions and we are more apt to either become disenchanted or reach for ever-increasing levels of opportunity.

As Managers, our transient tendencies are even more pronounced. We are usually in management as a result of us being wired to achieve. We have a desire for increasing levels of responsibility, influence, and compensation.

Often, we will struggle with the decision driven by fears that the grass is not greener on the other side, even though it appears that way. This chapter will help you decide if it is time to move on or not. It will not give you the answer but guide you towards self-examination of your situation by contemplating a series of questions.

When we change jobs, the antecedents are either positive, negative, or some combination of both. We will begin by attempting to understand the negative indicators that might prompt the pursuit of a new job.

Start by looking for some of the warning signs that may indicate it is time to move on or at a minimum, research your opportunities.

- **Have you become a clock watcher?** Or are you watching the clock more closely than you have in the past? If the answer is yes, and the clock appears to be moving slower while you are at work and faster while you are away from work, you should examine the cause of those actions. This is not to be confused with the individual who works 14 hours a day and has decided to dial back the intensity a bit in an effort to take care of one's health or family. It is at the other end of the spectrum where you are working closer to the minimum hours required or maybe even less than what is required.

- **Are you taking work home with you, either emotionally or mentally?** This is not the practice of "doing" work from home. Often there is both an expectation as well as a need for this to occur. This is the practice of not being able to disconnect from the problems/issues at work even when you want to. Most of us will think about work when we are not at work, however, if it moves towards an obsession, particularly when you don't want it to, you should consider it a warning sign. You have to determine if the obsession is caused by the job or by you. Some of us, are the obsessive type and will exhibit these behaviors no matter where we work. Think back! Have you felt this way in the past or is this new to you?

- **Do you catch yourself exhibiting anger more often?** This anger can be directed towards individuals and institutions or your situation. If your anger meter indicates that your anger is intensifying as well as a more frequent emotion, it may be time to examine your options. If you feel that work is the root cause of some sort of negative emotion you need to closely examine your situation. Depression, resentment, jealously, isolation, are all potential side effects of being dissatisfied with one's career. Be careful that these sentiments are not symptomatic of some sort of other issues. There is a tendency to blame our Employer for issues that are simply a result of our own actions.

Now that you have identified some Bonafede warning signs, and you confidently believe that these issues are based in how you are feeling towards your job and employer. With that in mind, ask yourself these questions that seek to help you understand your opinion of:

Work, Your Manager, Your Company

1. **Am I having an impact on the results in my corner of the company?** Do I feel effective, and do I get some sense of contentment as a result of my own effectiveness?

2. **Do I believe in my immediate leadership and am I learning from them?** Is communication good? Do I feel like I am being heard?

3. **Do I believe in the Leadership of the Company?** Generally, are we headed in the right direction? Are we responding to the fundamental threats that we are faced with?

If the answers are "no" in two of the categories, you should seriously explore your opportunities. If the answers are "no" across the board, it is clear that you have lost confidence in your future employment with this employer. In fact, it is likely that you are exhibiting behavior that is putting you at risk and may make the decision about your future out of your hands. Be careful!

Before you go any further you must force yourself to embark upon a heavy dose of self-reflection. You owe it to yourself to examine your role in the issues. How much of this is about attitude versus actions? Are you guilty of playing the role of a victim? Think of it this way: if one of your people were feeling the way you were feeling at this point (and you were happily employed) what advice would you provide? In virtually every circumstance, we are part of the problem. Even the slightest scintilla of the fault must be examined. Often it is far easier to change our attitude than to change our job.

Now let's look at positive reasons to move on....

- **You have topped out at your current Employer.** What do you define as the top? If you sincerely have promotion as a goal and it's for the right reason, then this can become a valid reason for leaving. Make sure to examine and try to determine what the top will look like in 3 years? And while you may have topped out, it's probably better described as boredom. What has changed since back when you were not bored? Maybe the steps needed to get to your goal are not aligned with your values. Another good reason for leaving. Ambition is a good thing for some people and a horrible thing for others.

- **You have accomplished close to everything that you were tasked with.** You have achieved your goals and objectives and the people you were privileged to lead are better off today than the day you arrived. You will have a positive legacy after your departure. Your job is finished and or you want to leave on top. If your feelings are accurate, you may get a tremendous retention offer from your current employer. If not, you have nothing to regret in leaving.

- **The offer from a prospective employer is substantially better than your current compensation.** If you are as good as was described in the previous bullet point, you should be getting offers that are close to or greater than a 20% increase in compensation at a minimum. Beyond the initial pay, benefits, and perks the potential of your future employer should be just as great if not greater than your current occupation.

- **Your Family or loved ones are supportive of the move.** They express confidence in you being successful in a different environment and any negative impact to them is acceptable.

- **You have been terminated.** While not a positive, it is for sure a reason for leaving, even though it might not be "your" reason.

Assuming you have now decided to explore your opportunity and leave if the right opportunity presents itself consider the following:

1. **Be careful with who you share your feelings.** Depending on your tactical approach to your search/departure, you may or may not want your current employer aware of either your dissatisfaction or your search for another job.

2. **If you do want your current employer to know, there are two basic methods...**

   Direct – Up Front – You simply tell them why you are contemplating a change. You will only do this if you want them to make an attempt to retain you. Note: This is a risky move. Don't bet on anything you're not willing to lose. You must have an accurate and confident opinion of yourself that is consistent with that of your Company. This opinion cannot simply be held by your immediate Supervisor, it must also be consistent with those that lead your Leader, as it is likely they are the ones who will have control over any retention offer.

   Indirect – You simply share this with someone who will pass it on, knowing that the information will get to those who matter. There are less subtle methods such as leaving your Resume in the copier or fax machine, however careless actions of that type may hurt your reputation when it comes to ones' opinion of your intelligence. This is not the recommended approach. It is far riskier, however, if you are considering this angle, it is likely there are trust issues already in existence.

3. **Be extremely mindful of your level of performance.** Once we decide to leave it is natural to disengage, even slightly. Fight the urge to think short-term. You owe it to your Company, staff,

peers, and customers to exhibit a high level of professionalism all the way to the end. Heading the opposite direction is normally easy to identify by those around you. As is always the case, you want as much control over your future as is possible. The element of surprise can be a critical component of a clean departure.

4. **Finding a job is easier while you have a job.** If at all possible, explore your options before quitting, unless you are financially situated to allow for a break in income. You are simply more attractive as a candidate while employed.

So, the planets have aligned, and it is absolutely clear it is time to offer up your resignation. As in everything, there is a right way and a wrong way to do things. Include the following guidelines and you will improve the chances of a harmonious breakup.

1. **Offer your resignation up verbally, followed by a written document.** Notifying by email, mail, telegram, Facebook, Instagram, text message, or skywriting is tacky. Manipulating the process so others find out about your departure before your immediate Supervisor does will serve no useful purpose.

2. **If you're leaving in anger, swallow that emotion and attempt to leave with the same amount of class that you had on your first day of work.** The only exception to this would be if you thought you were wronged in such a way that you will be seeking some sort of added compensation in the form of a Settlement of some sort. If that be the case, take your advice from an Attorney and not this book.

3. **Be diligent in your efforts to contribute to a smooth transition.** Provide the customary notification period which as a standard, is usually two weeks. If more time is needed and your future Employer is flexible in terms of your start date, make every effort to make the accommodation. Do as much as you can to help your customers, employees, peers, and Manager with the move to whoever is going to replace you. Resist any urges to bad-mouth anyone on your way out. Endorse your Employer and express confidence in the future of your soon-to-be former Employer.

The preceding is simply good advice that will help you avoid burning and bridges. The world is getting smaller and smaller. It is always good advice to limit the number of enemies or offended people that are viewable in our rear-view mirror.

Importantly, it is critical to consider as part of your decision to leave, where are you going? Staying a little longer might be necessary in order to find the right place to go to. It's a big, big decision. A mistake here can be painful.

Much like a Divorce, there must have been a time when you and your Employer were in love with each other, or at a minimum had mutually agreed upon needs. Hanging onto any ill will that you feel towards an Employer is unhealthy and will not serve you well in your next position or in life. Have a clean break and do your best to forgive, forget and move on.

CHAPTER FOURTEEN

MANAGING YOUR BOSS (IT IS MORE THAN DELEGATING UPWARDS)

If you happen to be my Boss and you are reading this, I hope you understand that none of the advice or opinions in this chapter have ever been utilized on you. Ok, maybe that is carry-over commentary from the previous chapter, however, if I have Managed a Boss. I would hope that he or she was aware that it was occurring.

When I say Manage Your Boss, by no means do I intend to insinuate you can create an environment where the hierarchy is reversed? The Boss is the Boss and while we can disagree and even not be aligned for brief periods of time, we must acknowledge that they are in charge. While we do not need to take the approach that the Boss is always right, our attempts to manage or delegate upwards should be motivated by our desire to perform at, or above expectations. This is in its purest form, merely an explanation of your role in the effort to collaborate for the good of the company. The disclaimer is now out of the way.

So, what is the process or act of Managing the boss? In brief, it can be defined as follows…

- Understanding the Boss's **needs** and responding to those needs.

- Assessing the **resources/strengths** of your Boss and finding out how to utilize them to the benefit of the company and your career.

Another one of those areas that is simple, but not easy. Let's dig a little deeper into each of these two points.

Needs – The vast majority of our Leader's needs that they will hope to meet through their teams, or as a byproduct of their team actions are mainly found in five categories. Those categories in their order of importance in my humble opinion are...

1. **Your Boss's key requirement should be the attainment of Results.** Even if they do not believe this is their primary purpose as your Leader, they will in their own way, say it is. As a result, your pursuit and attainment of your goals and objectives is the best way to manage your boss. If you are achieving results, they will probably leave you alone or interfere less than if you are coming up short. If your requests are perceived as benefiting the organization and or your Manager, they will be far more susceptible to any efforts by you to delegate upwards. So not only should you work hard to achieve your organization's or your department's goals, but you should also find subtle methods of making sure your Boss is aware of the achievements you have contributed to. Be careful, we typically are not as subtle as we think we are.

2. **Managers with vision and a desire to sustain results find satisfaction in developing their people.** Make sure that you are embarked on your own effort to develop and if your Manager suggests developmental activities, take full advantage of the offer. If you are seen as someone who is pursuing their potential more resources will be coming your way. Your Manager is doing this because he expects a return on his/her investment. Your development will help need number one results, and it will build upon needs number four and five. If your Manager is viewed as someone who is involved in the development of the Team, it will be good for career advancement, and recognition will undoubtedly be coming his way.

3. **Effective Managers are interested in building and sustaining relationships.** While these relationships may be limited to the work environment alone, many of our best friends are former colleagues. We tend to go through a lot with our contemporaries and loyalty and trust can be the foundation for lasting relationships.

Your boss is a lot like you and while he might keep a certain perimeter around his personnel life, he will find gratification in gaining your confidence.

4. **Many Managers fashion themselves to be on a path to career advancement.** Things that you do to help them further that cause will motivate them to create some level of reciprocation. In short, they will not mind helping you because you are helping them.

5. **Just like everyone in the world it is likely that your Boss has a need for recognition.** Recognition comes in many forms, some of it is in the form of compensation or promotion, both of which are outside of your direct control. When it comes to your Manager, however, your results may cause your Boss to get recognition, and hopefully, if that is the case, he is sharing or giving you and your team the credits you deserve. Remember that for your own team, the best way to get recognition is to give it. You can be the provider of recognition as well. Try your best to be sincere, this is one of many categories wherein honesty is the best approach.

Now let's talk about the strengths and resources of your Boss. Let's frame this discussion with those strengths that can help you in your career. I will do this by asking questions.

Is your boss…

- Is he/she good in front of your people?

- Does he/she compliment your approach by his presence?

- Is he/she analytical and able to see things that others miss?

- Does he/she have a tendency towards being creative?

- Does he/she seem to enjoy teaching/sharing knowledge?

- Is he/she organized in thought as well as processes?

- Is he/she good at time management?

- Is he/she willing to be an advocate for you and even a hammer when it is necessary?

- Does he/she enjoy contributing to your efforts, will he/she get involved?

Answering these questions and many more will cause you to contemplate who your Boss is and how he or she can help you. If you have a better understanding of their profile, it will help you decide what you can get help on, or what you can delegate. A big part of successful upward delegation is choosing what gets delegated.

Consider, what your Bosses' idiosyncrasies are. What are his or her pet peeves? Does he have any unwritten rules? Is he a morning person or an afternoon person? Consider all of these factors in your attempt to manage upward. For instance, if your Boss hates surprises (most do), work hard to keep him informed, error towards over communication. Your Boss may not feel good about speaking in front of groups, particularly when it is an impromptu communication, so avoid those instances as much as possible.

The absolute key to Managing your Boss is to assess the level of trust that exists between the two of you. If the trust is high, the task will be much easier. If it is low, you may want to consider shelving your plans to Manage or Delegate upward and be satisfied with simply having some measure of influence. If you are feeling good about your relationship you can utilize the following phrasing to open up the discussion on "getting help" which can be a way of cloaking the act of delegating up.

- I am not as good at this as you are, and I would really appreciate your help....

- You are really good at _____, could you teach me everything you know about it?

- I don't want you to do this for me, but I would like you to help me learn how to do it on my own.

- I would like you to show me how to do this, so I can do it myself next time.

- Your sponsorship and presence when we announce this strategy would mean a lot to the team and me.

- My team sincerely trusts you and I think our chances for success would be magnified by your presence next week....

- I hate saying this, and I think you would agree that you have not heard this from me too much in the past, but I am in need of some assistance.

- Right now, I am working on XYZ which I think we both believe should be the priority, can you think of another resource that could take on the task you just asked me to do? (You need a lot of trust built up between the two of you to attempt this one)

Let your people delegate up to you. I will repeat what I have said in other chapters, the key role of a Leader is to remove or diminish obstacles so that his team members can be successful. Be a resource to your team. Your Boss will observe it and may choose to mimic your good behavior. It's not just a good business practice it is good Karma as well.

Guard against delegating upwards too often or for small tasks. Ration any equity that you have in the bank that is leveraged for getting your Boss to do something for you. Over delegating increases the likelihood that the delegation will be well received and can ultimately lead to the following conclusion.

"If I have to do this, what do I need you for?"

Managing your boss or delegating upwardly is not always possible. You may be in a situation where it simply cannot be done. Your Boss believes you should have shown up to the party with all of the requisite skills and resources. He may be good at providing direction and managing up in his own environment but if you attempt it on him, disaster might strike. Realize this and do not attempt it. Even if you feel confident in your ability to Manage your Boss, do not do it too early in the relationship or too often.

Once you feel you are in a good spot in terms of your contribution to meet these needs you will be on your way. If your assessment of his or her strengths is accurate, you will have effectively brought those strengths to bear via layering them into your tactics and strategies. If all goes well you will be viewed as a team (your Boss and you) that exhibits good teamwork. A win for both of you.

CHAPTER FIFTEEN

YOU ARE ALWAYS THE BOSS

As Leaders, we are in positions where relationships develop with those we work with. For the most part, these relations can be a healthy part of the workplace environment. If you are a good Leader, relationship growth will be a natural byproduct of creating an atmosphere built on trust. Achieving results as well as growing together amid a crisis will create lasting bonds that will exist for years and maybe your entire life.

Often the simple test of time will cause relationships to develop and progress into what might be described as a friendship. Longevity, via a lengthy assignment, can be a catalyst for enduring relationships. In many cases, we spend more time with those we work with than we do with our own family.

Managers are even more guilty of this since they tend to work longer hours than non-Managers. How many of us spend 10 to 12 hours at work including commuting, arrive at home, and spend one hour with our family, followed by 3 hours of television and 8 hours of sleep?

While strong relationships are a key component to building a winning team, there is some peril associated with this phenomenon. Knowing about the potential risks in advance can help you manage the situation and limit any damage that might occur as a result of getting too close to your people.

It is important to remember that you are always the boss for some distinct reasons, most notably of which are....

1. **Even if your actions, as well as intentions, are pure, you will be accused by others of favoritism.** You may treat everyone equally,

however, if you are viewed as being closer to some of your people, you are bound to run into situations where others feel slighted and or jealous of the extra attention your so-called favorites receive. While in your mind and in reality, your expectations of these "favorites" as well as accountability is higher than it is for everyone else, you will be accused of providing preferential treatment. To some extent, it does not even matter if the accusation is true or not if it creates a level of mistrust.

2. **It can provide your critics with ammunition.** You may have people within your staff or even your peer group who do not agree with you. Their perspective may indeed be misguided and simply wrong; however, they will look for any seam in your approach to discredit you. The mere mention of favoritism to the right people will create enough of a distraction that it can hurt your plans or worse yet, derail your plans.

3. **Strong relationships can create blind spots for you.** The fact is that we often have trouble finding fault in those we love and or like. We have a natural tendency to surround ourselves with people who are like us and that share our values and interests. As Leaders, we face resistance to our approach from above, below, and beside us. While this resistance might be rare, we tend to seek comfort from those who agree with us, when we are lonely. Getting too close to our people can cause us to overlook their shortcomings or make excuses for their behavior and performance. Worse yet, it is difficult to self-diagnose our blind spots. It is simply the nature of the phenomenon, your blind to what you are blind to. I think I might have come up with a different version of "I don't know, what I don't know". We will see if it catches on.

There are a few preventive maintenance steps that you can take that will prevent you from stepping on this particular trap.

1. **Be particularly conscious of this issue early on in a new assignment.** This is when those who are more interested in managing their relationship with you, than their results, will look for an opportunity to exploit their very own (at least in

their mind's eye) magnetic personality. You may be in your most vulnerable position as well. Overwhelmed with learning the many new aspects of your new role while assessing the talent of your team. Who knows, you may even be getting to know a new boss. It can be a particularly lonely period of time. Not boring, but a period of time when you are susceptible to those who might take advantage of your good nature.

2. **Make a conscious effort to spread yourself around particularly with those activities that one might classify as social in nature.** Remembering that you are always under a microscope keep in mind how you are rationing instances such as going to lunch or dinner, having a cup of coffee, golfing, or going for a beer after work. I have known Managers who have even vacationed with their Direct Reports. Even though the Managers actions were pure and no favoritism was shown (in my opinion) others believed that favoritism indeed occurred. Yes, for those who know me. Guilty as charged.

3. **Work at maintaining and or developing friendships with people with who you do not work with.** This will limit your desire to spend too much time with people at work.

4. **Be leery of those who seek to accelerate the relationship.** Socializing with your team is a valuable and necessary part of building Esprit De Corp and gaining loyalty, however, you need to be on the lookout for those who seem to be pushing for the one-on-one experience. If you have your eyes open, you can see them a mile away. They want to get you alone on the golf course, over a meal, or at the bar and provide you with all the answers to your Department's issues. And they are typically a part of the solution in their humble opinion. Be proactive in organizing group events that allow you to spend time with a wide swatch of your team in a relaxed environment.

5. **Avoid compromising situations.** As Managers, we must strive to be beyond reproach. Being the drunkest one in the room is not the recommended approach for gaining loyalty. While some of

the group may believe it is great that the Boss let his hair down and was one of us for a few hours, there are far too many things that can go wrong when you are not in control. You can bet that you will be challenged when you are compromised and that your actions in these situations will get a lot of playback at the Water Cooler on Monday. There will be times when some may even lie about your behavior. As one of my Managers was fond of saying, "there is no reason to show your whole ass when half will do".

Do not take these pointers so literally that you are unable to have fun or allow people the opportunity to get to know you. Similar to most categories of Leadership, it is all about striking the proper balance or equilibrium. Awareness by itself should help you in the process of learning how to approach this opportunity.

Realize that you will make some mistakes in this regard. I sure did!

CHAPTER SIXTEEN

TERMINATIONS – SOME TIPS ON HOW TO PERFORM AN UNPLEASANT TASK

Communicating to someone the unexpected or even expected end of their employment or career can be a painful experience. It is almost always painful to the target of the termination and is often painful with those who are tasked to deliver the bad news.

Psychologists tell us that the sense of failure associated with losing a job is comparable to the death of a loved one or a divorce. Understandable, since it is a form of rejection that is extremely personal. Additionally, it creates serious doubts and concerns regarding one's future. Many working people have responsibilities that include providing for loved ones. The loss of a job may create justifiable fear about one's abilities to keep those commitments that are most sacred to us. Far too many of us find our self-worth wrapped up in our jobs. Unless we are in a position financially to only work because we want to, losing a job will be a frightening experience.

It is an ugly part of Leadership that very few find rewarding. There are actions and methods you can employ to make this process go smoother for both entities. Make no mistake, these are highly charged emotional exchanges, that can have an impact on the effectiveness of your organization, as well as your very own career.

The overall theme to your approach on terminations should have at its core, your desire to treat the subject of the termination with dignity and respect. Even for those who are terminated for cause, including such egregious infractions as embezzlement or discrimination, you should endeavor to treat them with class on their way out. It is probably a horrible comparison, but even our most heinous criminals are treated with some modicum of respect prior to their execution. Yeah, that was a horrible comparison, but you get the point.

In the hemisphere of terminations, there are two basic categories.

1.   Layoffs – Downsizing – Location Closures – Reduction in Work Forces.

2.   Terminations for Cause – Performance – Overt Act

In the first category, it is typically all about the actions and performance of the Company. Business conditions related to the performance of the company or the economy, often justify these actions. There are some instances, although they are relatively rare, wherein a group is downsized because of their collective performance, however, there is no need to blame these types of terminations on any individual(s).

You can expect the same range of emotions in terms of anger, denial, bargaining, etc. as you would with termination for cause. Losing your job, regardless of the reason is unpleasant and creates the same fear and uncertainty. It is however less of a personal attack on one's skills and abilities.

Termination for cause is far more personal. It will be related directly to the actions, mistakes, and in many cases abilities of the person being terminated. Consider for a moment that a layoff is a defensive move by the Employer, while a termination for cause is an offensive move. Far too often a termination for cause is a surprise, while a layoff often creates its own warning signs.

As a subset of a termination for cause, most actions can be separated into these two categories.

Overt Act – Theft, Under the influence of illegal drugs or alcohol, workplace violence, Sexual Harassment, gross negligence regarding safety rules. All good Human Resource manuals will have a thorough description of this category

Performance – Consistent and prolonged underachievement of goals and objectives combined with behaviors and actions that are counter to advise and expectations.

Most of the advice contained herein will be directed towards terminations for cause. This advice is applicable in many cases to both types of terminations.

The Prelude

Before any termination for cause is attempted you should have compiled thorough documentation. Even in the case of an overt act, you should protect yourself and your company by carefully detailing the chain of events that lead to the termination. Most terminations for cause related to performance, follow a **progressive discipline process.** These actions should have as a key component, precise documentation, much of which will be shared with the recipient of the discipline. Typically, this documentation will have the following components...

- The **area of concern** or substandard performance described–whenever possible attempt to quantify the issue using metrics that are well known in your business environment.

- What has been **asked of the Employee** in terms of goal achievement as well as changed behaviors? Again, make every attempt to quantify. The numbers are the goals while the behaviors are the specific actions that will contribute to the attainment of the goals.

- The **support that has been offered by the Employer** or Manager. We all want our Team Members to be successful. When there are issues, we should commit to helping by offering training, feedback, and whatever other resources can be employed to help

- The time frame that the discipline covers as wells as the ramifications of failure.

Most organizations will implement an interim step just prior to termination to ensure that there is both good documentation and no rush to judgment. This step can be referred to as a "suspension pending investigation".

A suspension of this nature allows you to gather all the facts, removes the Employee from the premises so that no further damage can occur and limits the exposure to actions that might occur from an employee who feels his or her employment is in jeopardy.

This allows you ample time to interview the employee who is in trouble and anyone else that may provide pertinent information related to the action. In light of your effort to treat everyone with dignity and respect, you should make every effort to limit the number of days that a suspension lasts. Typically, one to three days.

You should always confer with others before you terminate one of your Associates. It is likely that your organization has a protocol that involves your Human Resources Department as well as your immediate Manager. These additional opinions will act as a safeguard and help prevent you from making a mistake either procedurally or with the actual decision to terminate.

In essence, you need to be prepared. Small mistakes made during the preparation for termination can result in the action being overturned or reversed.

The Termination Conversation

You will want to take steps to ensure this communication allows for some level of privacy. There are two ways to look at this privacy issue.

1. **Privacy that shields the employee from fellow co-workers** so that the raw emotions that often are part of termination are not on display for everyone to witness.

2. **Privacy that shields the employee from co-workers but not the general public.** I knew some Managers who made a habit of terminating people in public places, such as a restaurant, hotel lobby, or even an airport terminal. This was typically utilized when a Manager was terminating another Manager. This method allows for some level of anonymity yet it is public enough that emotions might be kept in check by virtue of the fact so many people are in close proximity to the event. Of course, this does not always work. There can still be a "scene".

While you want to create the right environment, you should also remember to include a witness to the action. Typically, a fellow Manager. If you are working in a Collective Bargaining Agreement (Read Union) environment the employee may be allowed to have representation/witness as well.

Don't mistake this step for being part of the investigation. The information you need to gather to move forward on termination should occur before, not during the termination discussion.

It is conceivable that new information might be revealed during the termination conversation that changes the outcome. You should always listen! If follow-up is necessary, then do so. No need to cut corners.

Do not start the meeting via a friendly greeting. Starting with a "Hi how are you?" or "Good morning it is good to see you" may be well-intentioned, however, this is not a typical meeting, and you should set the tone appropriately. A simple "Hello Dave, please have a seat" or something like that will suffice.

Keep it short – You simply want to inform the Associate they are being terminated for cause. In one paragraph explain the infraction or performance category that is the basis for the action. In cases of progressive discipline, the Employee should be aware of the steps and processes that were taken to improve performance or modify behavior. In instances where you are terming for overt acts such as theft, violence, drug usage, etc., you will reference the actions and the requisite Company Policy that was violated. You want to keep this phase brief for two primary reasons.

1. The longer the explanation, the higher the likelihood that your discussion will deteriorate into an argument. You do not want to get into a pro-longed back and forth discussion during this phase. That may come later. The more you share, the higher the probability of making a mistake by saying the wrong thing. Stick to the facts and keep it brief.

2. There may be instances where you do not want your soon-to-be former Employee to know exactly what you know. That knowledge could be used against you and allows the Employee to conjure up

false explanations between the termination conversation and any type of appeal. You want the truth, and the truth is always easy to remember, therefore when all the facts come out during any subsequent appeal process, the Employee will have an opportunity, to tell the truth.

The exception to this rule would be some sort of new and unforeseen disclosure of information that was not revealed in prior discussions or investigatory efforts. An instance of that nature is worthy of follow-up. You will need to use your judgment and common sense in determining your reaction to new information.

In the case of a layoff, a brief description of the business rationale for the reduction in employees is appropriate, again do not get into a back-and-forth discussion.

Conclude the meeting by informing the employee of the next steps. In the case of a termination for cause, this will likely include an appeal process that may include multiple levels of appeal. The employee has the option of not pursuing appeal which happens more often than you would imagine.

If this conversation results in a mutual understanding and the employee agree to leave without an appeal, make every attempt to thank them for their contributions. Do not apologize, however you can express regret that the relationship ended this way.

Don't say: "I am sorry this happened, and I apologize for having to fire you"

Do say: "I regret how this has ended and I wish you well in your future endeavors"

It is ok to shake hands as you part company as the old saying goes, it's just business. A handshake happened more often than not.

And finally document the details of this discussion. After all, it may not be over even though it seems like it's over.

The Resources

At this point, you may be handing off the terminated employee to your Human Resources team or may partner with that person to discuss the next steps which may include some or all the following components

1. Collection of company assets, keys, computers, vehicles, etc.

2. An explanation of options pertaining to benefits via Cobra, or a company-supported severance agreement.

3. A process for collecting personal effects.

The Follow-up

Assuming the appeal process has been exhausted and the action to terminate upheld, spend some time considering what you have learned.

When someone is terminated for "Performance" there is blame that can be shared by both sides. What went wrong? Was something missed in the selection process? Were the training resources adequate? Where and how did the communication process break down? Consider what you may have learned from this incident and commit to not repeating your mistakes.

If you find that you are consistently terminating people and that your turnover of staff is higher than your peers or industry norms, you should strongly consider examining the root cause.

I had a new assignment that included a location with two very weak Managers. It's a long story, however, the inmates were running the asylum. Ultimately one of the Managers quit under pressure and the other took a demotion. I replaced these two weak Managers with one strong Manager.

Prior to him taking over this workgroup of approximately 30 people, I explained to him the magnitude of the problem he was inheriting. I explained that you have a relatively large group within the 30 team members who have a combination of poor results as well as a horrible attitude. They appear to be actively recruiting others within the workgroup to join their race to the bottom. I refer to them as the

Magnificent 7. It needs to be addressed. Hopefully, you can get them to come around, if not, you are going to have to get rid of them. That was about 16 years ago as of this writing. Within two years, the problem was solved because of some changed attitudes as well as terminations for cause. The Manager remains there to this day. Sometimes the carnage is necessary.

On the other hand, if your style and approach are the primary catalysts for repeated terminations you could become the target of the next meeting of this nature. I seriously doubt that is the case. It has been my observation that people who are attempting to improve themselves through reading or any other means are not typically the type of Manager who "creates" unnecessary terminations.

CHAPTER SEVENTEEN

SAFETY & MORALE –
THE INTER-RELATION

This chapter will not give you the answer to the issues related to the theory that morale has an impact on safety. I am merely attempting to expose you to the theory so that you consider it as you operate your business. The key to good morale can be found in other chapters within this book as well as other books and experiences. It is my belief that if you anticipate the impact of your decisions on morale as well as your business results, including safety, you will become a more effective Leader.

A high injury or accident rate can be the canary in the coal mine in terms of a warning system that some other issues exist in a business. Examination of these trends should be a part of the due diligence process for Mergers and Acquisitions.

Every company has or should have some sort of safety program in place that ensures that a proactive approach is taken towards the safety of Associates as well as the safety of civilians who come in contact with the Company. Safety issues can cost you money via injuries as well as accidents. The expense in this category is not limited to those who are hurt as a result of an accident. There is also expense tied to accidents that damage property or the environment that can be even more costly.

While an unbudgeted expense is hard to swallow, it can be equally hard on an organization emotionally when people are injured or in some cases killed.

While the hard costs are relatively easy to quantify and they by themselves justify a proactive approach, the soft costs maybe even higher. When injuries occur, people miss work, those who are left behind must fill the breach and the whole experience can be a major distraction for people beyond the ones that are hurt. Customer relations may be interrupted and the shift in attention can have a huge impact on efficiencies.

Injuries/Accidents can affect the reputation and image of the company as well.

Simply put, it is important to provide for the safety of your Associates. It is one of the sacred responsibilities of a Leader. There may well be inherent dangers in various job functions throughout your organization, however, it is your duty to minimize the dangers and be ever vigilant in your approach to find a safer way to get the job done.

How robust your plans will be, will depend on the frequency of injuries or potential for injuries. Workers Compensation expenses can easily ruin a year financially in many companies. Like normal Health Care costs, costs to treat injured workers have tracked the same upward curve that our health care costs have achieved.

Similar to most insurance costs, a bad day, month or year can stay with you for many, many years in the form of higher premiums and in some cases added attention to various regulatory agencies such as OSHA.

There are Companies or Consultants out there that will cost you significant amounts of money as they attempt to help you reduce your expense related to injuries and accidents. They will come in and give you basic training on lifting, driving a truck, forklift, or any other piece of machinery you might utilize. They will study the ergonomics of your various job functions and may even show you how the principles of martial arts can make for a safer work environment. It's an entire industry on to itself.

All of them will attempt to raise awareness and help you to create a culture of safety in your company. All these efforts are worthwhile and can help your organization, however like any effort where Consultants are asked to pitch in on, the success will rely on the execution of the follow-up efforts once the Consultants have left your property.

The factor that few people discuss when it comes to Safety is the effect morale can have on an organization's injury rate. We all believe that a certain percentage of injuries and accidents are attitudinal. Some believe the percentage of attitudinal injuries is in the 10% range, while others will argue that it is approaching 50%. It is not difficult to feign a soft tissue injury such as a muscle pull. The contributing factors or components of these "Bad Attitudes" probably fall under one of the following categories.

1. **Lack of personnel job security** – When an Associate feels threatened or insecure, this feeling can often be the catalyst for an injury, real or imagined. Throughout my 30 years in Management, I witnessed several injuries that occurred shortly before (Or in some cases after) a termination was scheduled to occur, or a layoff notice was about to be announced.

2. **Lack of faith in the Company** – Many companies go through tough times and their employees do not lose one iota of faith in the company or the Leadership. While others can magnify the degree of difficulty simply by ignoring the necessity to keep people informed. They want to hear that you have a firm grasp on what is wrong with the company as well as some sort of plan for recovery. If they feel a part of the solution, all the better.

3. **Lack of faith, respect, and willingness to follow their Leader** – Sometimes this can be a simple personality conflict. Sometimes, the employee is just misplaced and sometimes the Leader is misplaced. If anything, close to a majority is feeling this way, in any one workgroup, a change is in order.

I witnessed the phenomenon of the interrelation between morale and safety on more than one occasion. At times it was from a distance and other times it was up close and personal. The following examples may be like your own experiences.

1. **During my years in a Unionized environment, we could anticipate (and therefore budgeted for) an uptick in injuries in the year where we were negotiating the Collective Bargaining Agreement.** As we got towards the end of the process and the

threat of a strike appeared possible (we always avoided a strike) a number of employees realized that Workers Comp was a more lucrative form of compensation than the $50 per week their Union Strike fund would provide them.

2. **During recessions or high unemployment periods, our businesses suffered along with most other corporations.** I repeatedly witnessed examples on both sides of the equation. Those that were proactive in communicating the issues and solutions realized no impact in injury/accident frequency. In fact, in some cases, it brought the front line and Leadership together as a team fighting a common cause. Those that did not experience a spike in incidents.

3. **On more than one occasion, I made a change in Managers by removing a poor Leader and inserting a good Leader.** In virtually every instance the safety record improved. This was not solely because the new and improved Manager placed more emphasis on Safety, which was true, however the big gains were the reduction of attitudinal injuries. Because there was a good feeling towards their Leader, the Associates were more attentive to the safety rules and worked through small aches and pains that would have provided them with some time off in the prior regime.

4. **A good environment is contagious.** You can tell when a group of Associates is having a little fun at work and when they were not. You can almost feel it when you enter the room. If the workforce enjoys being around each other and their Leader, there will always be a correlation in the injury and accident rate. If employees feel they are a part of the process and contribute in such a way that they feel ownership they will create their own positive momentum and even peer pressure that will focus them on safer behavior and results as well as improved business results.

Of course, there are times when you must move forward with unpopular news or a strategy that creates some grumbling. The pursuit of the Companies or your workgroups objectives is absolutely the top priority. While you must do your best to represent the rationale behind your decisions, there will certainly be days when you must make some lonely decisions.

If you, do it right, you will have built up some equity with your team that can be called upon to help you get through difficult transitions. This equity is especially useful when you are attempting to either overcome your own mistakes or mistakes made by those above you. Use this equity properly and these momentary transitions will not have a negative effect on your Safety results.

CHAPTER EIGHTEEN

CULTURE – UNDERSTANDING – CREATING/CHANGING

Our world is becoming more and more diverse with each passing year. Despite some resistance to the blending of cultures, it no doubt will continue this arch for the foreseeable future.

Throughout your career, there is a good chance that you will be exposed to cultures that are different than what you have experienced in the past. I believe it is an underrated benefit of a career that results in promotions and/or job changes because of relocation.

And while there is a distinction between a person's culture and an organization's culture, they often overlap. For instance, in parts of the Middle East, Religion is not only a part of society's culture, but it also has a big impact on work culture, while in the US evidence of religious beliefs is not as prevalent in the workplace.

Even within an organization, there can be differences. I had a Region that included a location with a mostly Hispanic workforce. Thirty miles away, the workforce was predominately African American. In another direction, the distribution center was a predominantly Caucasian workforce. There were three distinct personalities for each workgroup.

And while the rules and policies were all the same, the behavior and habits of those populations were different. Music, food, humor, slang, and even friendliness were distinctly different.

My assignment in Dubai in the United Arab Emirates was very diverse. At the time, 92% of the population were Ex Pats. That's right, only 8% of the public was native to the country.

After about 18 months in Dubai, I organized a surprise birthday party for my wife. There were 16 couples, 32 people who attended. In that group, 15 countries were represented. As I recall, it included, Lebanese, Syrian, British, Irish, Austrian, Italian, Mexican, Russian, Brazilian, Sri Lankan, Indian, Pakistani, German, Canadian, and American. That evening was in the top five in terms of experiences during our 8 years there.

With this experience in mind, I offer up the following advice starting with personal culture. I believe it applies within the US as well as other countries.

Do the following.

- **Seek understanding** – If you cannot do it in advance of your new assignment, it will need to be via on-the-job experience. I had about a 3-month transition period prior to going to Dubai. I used that time to read books that specifically addressed the nuances of the culture there. I networked with people who either lived there at the time or in the recent past. We were typical Americans. We did not have a Passport and had only traveled to Canada and Mexico before Dubai. We had a lot to learn due to our isolation and lack of experience. Keep a positive attitude about it all and it will be a wonderful adventure for you. If your assignment is domestic similar efforts can be pursued to go in with your eyes wide open.

- **Focus on observing.** Remember 2 ears one mouth. In this regard, the ears need to be your primary tool along with your eyes. The mouth should primarily be used to seek clarity in the beginning.

- **Embrace it,** this does not mean you need to convert to it, however, be open to it. Being exposed to learning and experiencing another culture even in the workplace will be enriching. It will give you a perspective that you might not otherwise be able to attain.

- **Apply your learning.** Understanding and observing should convert to learning. Look for opportunities to apply this knowledge. Generally, people appreciate it if you try to learn about their culture. If you can learn a little bit of their language, all the better.

This effort will go a long way towards opening the dialogue.

- **Don't be a Chameleon.** Adjust yes, a wholesale change no. It most likely will be viewed as insincere. Particularly if it is only temporary.

- **When suggesting an idea avoid saying "At my former employer, we did it this way…."** Better to say, "I suggest we do it this way". Or "have you thought about doing it this way". There could be resentment towards the place you came from or the company you came from. Generally, if others are interested in knowing how it was done somewhere else, they will ask that specifically "How did you do this at X or in X?

Why do all this? Besides being good for you, it will be good for the business. A warm welcoming approach to adjusting to your atmosphere will build the sense of teamwork as well as trust that will be important to your success.

The principles above will give you a foundation for effecting change in the culture. You begin by seeking understanding. Then you either change or create depending on the situation.

> **Changing** a company culture is far more complicated and riskier than creating one. Be subtle and go slow, in most cases, unless you have been assigned to a group that essentially needs to be burned to the ground. (Figure of speech).

> **Creating** one in a newly formed company is much easier to produce, yet just as difficult to maintain as the culture existing in a mature company.

The endeavor to change a culture cannot be adequately covered in a book that has as a guiding principle, brevity.

I will however provide my view in bullet point form as it relates to creating a culture in a new company. I did it once, starting as the first employee and leaving after 1,100 people had joined our ranks. after 6 and half years.

1.   **All the tips above on learning a societal culture apply.** Listen,

observe, study seek advice.

2. **Know who you are and where you want to take the team.** Articulate what you want to be known for first, followed by the steps you need to take to get there.

3. **Let the team know who you are.** After you break the ice, share with them facts that they do not know about you. Have a leadership philosophy that you can articulate to others.

4. **Try to understand where your team wants to go.** What are they known for and where do they want to go? Try to find commonality. Show them you can compromise. Your chances of succeeding go way up if you collaborate on company direction. I knew more than one Manager who appeared to be wanting to be known as someone who is a good golfer. Golfing was part of every week's activity, sometimes more than once a week. You know the kind of guy. He can be seen compulsively practicing his golf swing, without a golf club, during breaks from meetings.

5. **When you feel you have comfortably figured out points 1, 2, 3, and 4, or at least come close to figuring it out, share your observations with your team.** Inbound their feedback and adjust if necessary.

6. **Work together on both your Organization Vision Statement and or Mission Statement.** This is one activity that is improved by getting outside assistance in constructing it.

7. **Get help.** While this book might help you, this chapter by itself will not. You need more help than that. Read more! Seek counsel from those who have effectively changed culture in the past,

Seems like the Universe dictates those opportunities to create a culture, happen in the latter half of a person's career. With many notable exceptions in Silicon Valley, we are usually somewhat seasoned by the time the challenge of creating a culture comes our way.

CHAPTER NINETEEN

NEPOTISM
THERE ARE THE RULES,
THEN THERE ARE THE RULES

This is one of those sections of our work life that we tend to ignore until it becomes an issue. We are typically not proactive in our approach to Nepotism. Depending on your organization, it is an area where rules are bent or broken, and the familiar "grandfather" option is repeatedly used.

After all. there is nothing more emotional than our love for our family and that is the way it should be. This genuine sentiment can cloud our better judgment and it is close to impossible to be objective when we are considering factors that affect our loved ones.

The term nepotism with its roots found in the Middle Ages with the Catholic Church is interpreted in a few different ways. Some believe it is the act of showing favor to a relative who is undeserving or not qualified, unworthy of whatever it is that has been given to the relative, whether it be position, power, or money.

I worked with a mid-level Manager who believed nepotism only occurred when an Associate formally complained about a situation involving two relatives. This is the "tree falling in a forest when nobody is there to hear it, theory". Yes, it was two of his employees in his department that were creating problems for some of my team.

Most Policy manuals take a more narrow and specific approach to defining Nepotism. While there is currently no Federal law that bars the practice of Nepotism, there are some states where guidelines have been legislated.

It is more prevalent in small companies than it is in large ones. I believe that the limited chance of success for relatives working in the same company is easier in smaller companies. Particularly those that are family-owned and operated.

There have been instances where an Employee either complained to the EEOC or sued based upon discrimination because of Nepotism.

Ergo the need and existence for Anti-Nepotism rules/policies in many of our larger companies whether they be private or public.

Anti-Nepotism rules vary from one company to the next so you will first need to understand what your Company's "official" point of view is. You will probably find something that has some or most of the following components.

1. Relatives cannot be hired into or work within the same location.

2. Relatives cannot work within the same function/department regardless of location.

3. Relatives cannot be able to Supervise or Influence the performance of a Relative or a Relatives staff.

4. The definition of a relative is, spouse, parent, grandparent, child, in-law, cousin, aunt, uncle, sibling.

In some cases (and this is where the rule-bending begins) an instance of relatives working together will be grandfathered. That is to say, that the instance existed before the implementation of the Policy and while it will not be allowed to be repeated, it will let it exist in its current form. An example would be in the case where a company is purchased or merges with another Company where the Anti Nepotism rules are not consistent.

At times relationships will develop to the point of marriage or some other type of commitment that brings up the issue of nepotism. Often policies are in place to deal with this phenomenon. Even requiring one of the pair to transfer or resign.

It has been my repeated observation that every effort should be made to avoid the practice of Nepotism. While I have witnessed some exceptions, I have seen far more instances where it created difficulties versus benefits particularly when one of the related is a Manager.

If you were to employ a relative, even if you are perfectly pure in your actions and leadership of this individual, you will at some point be accused of favoritism. This accusation may indeed be false, yet the environment will suffer.

I have repeatedly witnessed instances where one or both relatives are terminated for cause. Similarly, I have witnessed careers derailed either temporarily or on a permanent basis because of fallout from Nepotism. The inappropriate actions of a relative can be the source of great embarrassment that can have a lasting effect on one's reputation.

In the United Arab Emirates, the practices and policies were quite different. The country's government is a constitutional monarchy, was run by the "Royal" family and to some extent, there was a degree of tribalism that carried over into the business world as well.

In the first company I worked for, I think I might have been the only member of the 6,500 staff that did not have a relative working for the company. I think we might have employed large parts of villages originating on the sub-continent. It was pervasive. It was not only accepted but expected. The frequency of issues included clusters of family members that were considered powerful and dangerous.

When there are clusters of relatives working in a company there is a belief that a Mafia has been formed. People believe the relatives represent a power base that does not necessarily have their best interests in mind.

How was this justified? Beyond the loyalty and love reasons, some believed that the rationale included the following…

1.   Generally, relatives will only recommend good relatives as they don't want to be embarrassed.

2.   Relatives keep each other accountable.

3.   It contributes to a family atmosphere. Literally!

I will admit, that all 3 of these justifications were true to some extent. Not sure if the good, outweighed the bad.

In the Company that I was asked to start, we made every attempt to follow the first 3 rules listed above. As we got bigger, I believe there was a lot more nepotism than was reported. Occasionally, I would come across an instance of it that was not previously disclosed.

As stated elsewhere in this book, a Manager must make every effort to be beyond reproach. Allowing the hiring of a relative provides unnecessary ammunition real or imagined for those who might want you to fail.

Again, even if you are pure in your actions, it will be natural that others will not share the truth with you or the relative who is in Management regarding your relative's performance. It well may be a point of discussion around the water cooler however you may not be privy to the rumors and innuendo until it is too late.

The relative who is second to arrive at a Company, either has a good reputation to live up to or in some rare instances, a negative legacy to overcome. You must know that the Boss's relative will be treated differently, so proceed at your own risk.

Hopefully, it is not too prevalent in your organization and you will be able to avoid this type of difficult environment during your time as a Manager.

CHAPTER TWENTY

DIFFERENTIATION

In nature, the process of differentiation is in its simplest form, the separating of a mixture of materials partially or completely. An example, the cooling and solidification of magma into two or more different rock types or in the gradual separation of originally homogeneous earth into crust, mantle, and core.

In business, it is very similar as well as important. This importance affects two primary segments of our work life.

They are…

- The **competitive differentiation** in the eyes of your customer in terms of the perceived value of your goods and services.

- The **perceived differentiation** in your own personal performance, skill set, and style.

Helping you differentiate your product, as well as your persona, is difficult. The drive for that effort will need to be internally driven. What I can do is spend some time explaining why it is so important, which will hopefully create a desire and motivation to seek differentiation. Remembering along the way, to seek the correct type of differentiation. Serial Killers after all, in the end, are viewed as different, but in a very negative way of course.

The Importance of Competitive Differentiation

Every business in the world attempts to separate itself from its competitors. The most obvious point of difference is typically **price** followed closely by **service**. The information age has raised the importance of differentiation to new levels as your customers have more access to competitive price comparisons, as well as the perceived level of service your company can provide.

The exception to this is counterfeiters, who do the exact opposite. And while they usually are breaking laws and regulations, there must be instances where it is commercially successful. They either try to replicate your product 100% or a portion of it. I suppose one should take it as a compliment, but I don't.

In terms of pricing architecture, there are many websites that will quickly perform price comparisons, some of which are quite sophisticated and widely used.

Likewise, there are a number of sites that are only a few keystrokes away that will provide "End Users" opinions of their experience with you and your competitors leading to a perceived quality differential.

Customers are just like we are, in that they tend to complain more often than compliment. Furthermore, those that complain are typically far more passionate than those who compliment. A single customer who might have a large following or fan base can with their smartphone do untold damage to your company's reputation as well as performance.

As a result, you must be proactive on two fronts. First and foremost are your efforts to **constantly improve the customer experience.** Your execution here will be the basis for those opinions.

I was often asked particularly to be the media, "what is your point of differentiation or Unique Selling Proposition USP?" In the UAE my answer went something like this… "It is difficult to do in the bottled water business, where your product is supposed to be odorless, colorless, and tasteless. Considering that we believe there is some nuance to the taste that some can detect, but beyond that, it comes down to our commitment to quality products and service, which we believe is unsurpassed".

A long time ago, someone said "A customer's opinion of a company is equal to their single worst experience with that company". While you might be able to overcome this supposed axiom through a long history of world-class service, a bad customer experience can eat away at any equity you have established in this area. It is a setback you undoubtedly will want to avoid.

As both a company and an individual, you must **know who you are!** You must understand both your weaknesses and strengths. Of course, you will spend a lot of time improving upon those areas of opportunity, however, you must have a firm grip on your overall strategy as well as how you compare to your competitor. In some cases, you will consciously choose not to compete in certain service areas.

Let me illustrate…

I have flown Southwest Airlines for 20 years with an average number of round trips per year of 38. Southwest clearly understands who they are! While they are constantly seeking improvement to their processes and customer experience, they also know that they are the "No Frills" airline. There is no first-class seating on any of their planes. You can however, "earn" or "pay" your way into some level of privilege. They also understand that most of the customer experience is created by the Associates of Southwest. One could argue that their Flight Attendants are the hardest working in the industry while also being the happiest. Southwest has gotten this way through a conscious effort. They have been known to hire based upon one's humor competency.

Sure, they have their detractors, however, very few domestic airlines if any, come close to matching their financial performance. They have a firm grip on their niche and are easy to differentiate.

For many years they were known for having the ugliest planes in the sky, The combination of colors was unforgettable and indeed created a differentiation that grew the Brand. A bold move.

It is clear that Southwest embraces three of the key ingredients to differentiating your product/service.

1.   **Seeking constant improvement** – they tinker with everything in an effort to accomplish improvement in service or efficiency. Efficiency improvement supports their main point of

differentiation – LOW-COST PROVIDER.

2. **Effectively tell your story** – All the differentiation in the world does you no good if you are ineffective at educating your customers, as well as potential customers on why you are different. They have a large advertising budget that facilitates this effort. It is clear to see that they are consistently attempting to educate.

3. **Be a bold innovator** – Part and parcel of this effort are knowing and listening to both your customers and your employees. Take chances yet ensure that these are calculated risks. Test them in isolation whenever possible and make sure you have a good execution plan. Many fantastic ideas have failed as a result of poor execution. While copying a competitor can be a useful component of improving performance, if your competitor is not occasionally copying your innovations, it is a clear sign you are bogged down and in danger of being left in the dust.

Many of us will say that we are not able to make the decisions that will create differentiation. These arguments can be expressed through comments such as "I am only responsible for the execution, they come up with the ideas and innovations and I simply carry out the plan".

Personal differentiation will be arrived at as a result of excelling in certain areas. You can become a specialist with a reputation that might look like this.

1. He/ She is good at turning around a substandard operation. In fact, better at that than improving a well-run operation.

2. He/ She often brings a creative solution to a problem.

3. He/ She is a good communicator and because of that he/she does well at getting things done through others.

4. He/ She is really good with numbers which causes his/her to be above average in terms of analysis.

5. He/ She is good at judging talent whether it is with existing team members or potential new hires.

6.   His/ Her style causes an open dialogue. People feel valued in his/ her group and that atmosphere contributes to his/her success.

7.   His/ Her contacts in the industry are unsurpassed and he/she uses this network to build the business.

8.   He/ She has the unique ability to be extremely firm, yet fair.

9.   That Guy/ Gal, always has the customer's best interest in mind. He/ She seems to have a supernatural ability to predict customer behavior.

10. There is nobody in this industry that knows as much as he/she does. He/ She leverages his/her long service record and past accomplishments for present and future success.

To come up with this list of ten people, I simply thought of Managers that I knew throughout the years and considered what their real-life point of differentiation was.

Differentiation is complicated in many ways. On the one hand, we are taught to comply and march in lock-step with others. At the same time, many of us want to take our own path, whenever possible.

It is hard to stand out in a crowd and sometimes you should not want to. While this may largely be true, I believe that one can still differentiate our own little sphere of influence. We do this by being good Leaders. We do this by improving in the areas that contribute to performance, many of which are in other chapters in this book. And often, because of our performance and the performance of our Teams, we will be able to influence and affect the effort to differentiate our product/service and even pricing on occasion.

About the Author

Jay Andres is the former CEO of Mai Dubai Bottled Water in the United Arab Emirates. He was Mai Dubai's first employee. Within 6 years Jay and his team built a factory and business that is doing over $100 million in annual revenue.

Jay was there for the onboarding of over 1000 employees within 6 years. Under his leadership, a factory of 50,000 square feet was built and then expanded to over 420,000 square feet.

The foundation was built, and the company has continued to thrive to this day. Jay continues to serve on the Board of Directors.

Before Dubai, he worked in the Bottled Water Industry in the United State for 31 years. His assignments took him to progressively more challenging roles, throughout most of the Western States.

While he came upon the Sales and Distribution side of the business, he transitioned to General Management expanding his skill set to include Marketing, Finance, Human Resource as well as Factory Operations.

Jay and his wife of 45 years live in Phoenix Arizona and enjoy recalling all their fond memories of their time together and making new memories every day.

Made in the USA
Coppell, TX
18 March 2023

14382629R00066